BiteSize Python for Absolute Beginners

As an introduction to Python, this book allows readers to take a slow and steady approach to understanding Python code, explaining concepts, connecting programming with real-life examples, writing Python programs, and completing case studies.

While there are many books, websites, and online courses about the topic, we break down Python programming into easily digestible lessons of less than 5 minutes each, following our BiteSize approach. Each lesson begins with a clear and short introduction to the topic. This gives you a strong base to start from and gets you ready for deeper learning. Then, you will see coding demonstrations that show the ideas discussed. These examples are simple and useful, helping you really understand the concepts. You'll then practice tasks at different difficulty levels, so you can test your knowledge and increase your confidence. You'll also play with case studies to solve real-world problems. Tips are included to show how you can incorporate generative AI into your learning toolkit, using it for feedback, practice exercises, code reviews, and exploring advanced topics. Recommended AI prompts can help you identify areas for improvement, review key concepts, and track your progress.

This book is designed for absolute beginners with no prior programming experience. It is ideal for individuals with busy schedules or limited time for studying.

Chapman & Hall/CRC

The Python Series

About the Series

Python has been ranked as the most popular programming language, and it is widely used in education and industry. This book series will offer a wide range of books on Python for students and professionals. Titles in the series will help users learn the language at an introductory and advanced level, and explore its many applications in data science, AI, and machine learning. Series titles can also be supplemented with Jupyter notebooks.

Statistics and Data Visualisation with Python
Jesús Rogel-Salazar

Introduction to Python for Humanists
William J.B. Mattingly

Python for Scientific Computation and Artificial Intelligence
Stephen Lynch

Learning Professional Python Volume 1: The Basics
Usharani Bhimavarapu and Jude D. Hemanth

Learning Professional Python Volume 2: Advanced
Usharani Bhimavarapu and Jude D. Hemanth

Learning Advanced Python from Open Source Projects
Rongpeng Li

Foundations of Data Science with Python
John Mark Shea

Data Mining with Python: Theory, Applications, and Case Studies
Di Wu

A Simple Introduction to Python
Stephen Lynch

Introduction to Python: with Applications in Optimization, Image and Video Processing, and Machine Learning
David Baez-Lopez and David Alfredo Báez Villegas

Tidy Finance with Python
Christoph Frey, Christoph Scheuch, Stefan Voigt and Patrick Weiss

Introduction to Quantitative Social Science with Python
Weiqi Zhang and Dmitry Zinoviev

Python Programming for Mathematics
Julien Guillod

Geocomputation with Python
Michael Dorman, Anita Graser, Jakub Nowosad and Robin Lovelace

BiteSize Python for Absolute Beginners: With Practice Labs, Real-World Examples, and Generative AI Assistance
Di Wu

For more information about this series please visit: https://www.routledge.com/Chapman--HallCRC-The-Python-Series/book-series/PYTH

BiteSize Python for Absolute Beginners

With Practice Labs, Real-World Examples, and Generative AI Assistance

Di Wu

CRC Press
Taylor & Francis Group
Boca Raton London New York

CRC Press is an imprint of the
Taylor & Francis Group, an **informa** business

A CHAPMAN & HALL BOOK

First edition published 2026
by CRC Press
2385 NW Executive Center Drive, Suite 320, Boca Raton FL 33431

and by CRC Press
4 Park Square, Milton Park, Abingdon, Oxon, OX14 4RN

CRC Press is an imprint of Taylor & Francis Group, LLC

ISBN: 978-1-032-86488-4 (hbk)
ISBN: 978-1-032-86485-3 (pbk)
ISBN: 978-1-003-52772-5 (ebk)

DOI: 10.1201/9781003527725

Typeset in Nimbus Roman
by KnowledgeWorks Global Ltd.

To my wife.

Contents

List of Figures   xvii

List of Tables   xix

Foreword   xxi

Preface   xxiii

Author Bios   xxvii

SECTION I   Python Fundamentals

CHAPTER	1 ▪ Introduction to Python	3
1.1	WHAT IS PYTHON?	3
1.2	WHY PYTHON?	4
1.3	SCRIPT VERSUS INTERACTIVE PYTHON	4
1.4	WHY INTERACTIVE PYTHON?	5
1.5	JUPYTER	6
1.6	LOCAL OR CLOUD	7
1.7	LEARNING PYTHON	8

CHAPTER	2 ▪ Input and Output	10
2.1	HELLO, WORLD!	10
2.1.1	Demonstration	10
2.1.2	Practice	11
2.2	SINGLE OR DOUBLE	11
2.2.1	Explanation	11
2.2.2	Demonstration	12
2.2.3	Practice	12
2.3	TRIPLE QUOTATIONS	13
2.3.1	Explanation	13

2.3.2   Practice   14

2.4   PRINT MULTIPLE VALUES   15

    2.4.1   Demonstration   15

    2.4.2   Practice   15

2.5   INTERACT WITH GENAI   15

2.6   GET INPUTS   16

    2.6.1   Demonstration   16

    2.6.2   Practice   16

2.7   COMBINE `PRINT()` AND `INPUT()`   17

    2.7.1   Explanation   17

    2.7.2   Demonstration   17

    2.7.3   Practice   17

2.8   INTERACT WITH GENAI   18

CHAPTER   3 ▪ Variables   19

3.1   WHAT ARE VARIABLES   19

    3.1.1   Explanation   19

    3.1.2   Practice   20

3.2   NAMING RULES   20

    3.2.1   Explanation   20

    3.2.2   Practice   21

3.3   DATA TYPES   21

    3.3.1   Explanation   21

    3.3.2   Practice   22

3.4   DATA TYPES CONVERT   23

    3.4.1   Explanation   23

    3.4.2   Demonstration   23

    3.4.3   Practice   24

3.5   INTERACT WITH GENAI   25

CHAPTER   4 ▪ Operations   26

4.1   ASSIGNMENT OPERATIONS   26

    4.1.1   Explanation   26

    4.1.2   Practice   27

4.2   ARITHMETIC OPERATIONS   27

    4.2.1   Explanation   27

    4.2.2   Demonstration   28

	4.2.3	Practice	29
4.3	RELATIONAL OPERATIONS		30
	4.3.1	Explanation	30
	4.3.2	Practice	30
4.4	LOGICAL OPERATIONS		31
	4.4.1	Explanation	31
	4.4.2	Practice	32
4.5	INTERACT WITH GENAI		34

CHAPTER	5 ▪ String		36
5.1	WHAT IS STR?		36
	5.1.1	Explanation	36
	5.1.2	Thinking	36
5.2	STRING CREATION		36
	5.2.1	Demonstration	37
5.3	STRING ACCESS		37
	5.3.1	Demonstraton	37
	5.3.2	Practice	39
5.4	STRING SLICING		40
	5.4.1	Demonstration	41
	5.4.2	Practice	42
5.5	STRING CONCATENATION		42
	5.5.1	Demonstration	42
5.6	STRING FORMAT		43
	5.6.1	Demonstration	43
	5.6.2	Practice	45
5.7	USEFUL FUNCTIONS		46
	5.7.1	Demonstration	46
	5.7.2	Practice	48
5.8	INTERACT WITH GENAI		51

CHAPTER	6 ▪ Case Studies of Python Fundamentals		52
6.1	SIMPLE CHECK OUT		52
6.2	TIPS SPLIT		53
6.3	COMPOUND INTEREST		54

SECTION II Flow Control and Functions

CHAPTER	7 ▪ Branching	57
7.1	OPTIONAL BRANCHING	57
7.1.1	Demonstration	58
7.1.2	Practice	59
7.2	ALTERNATIVE BRANCHING	60
7.2.1	Demonstration	60
7.2.2	Practice	61
7.3	MULTIPLE BRANCHING	62
7.3.1	Demonstration	63
7.3.2	Practice	64
7.4	CASE STUDIES OF BRANCHING	66
7.4.1	What day is today?	66
7.4.2	Tax calculator	66
7.4.3	A simple calculator	67
7.4.4	Taxi fare calculator	68
7.5	INTERACT WITH GENAI	69

CHAPTER	8 ▪ Repetition	70
8.1	CONDITION-BASED REPETITION	70
8.1.1	Explanation	70
8.1.2	Demonstration	71
8.1.3	Practice	72
8.2	COUNT-BASED REPETITION	74
8.2.1	Explanation	74
8.2.2	Demonstration	75
8.2.3	Practice	76
8.3	MAGIC CONTROL	78
8.3.1	Demonstration	78
8.3.2	Practice	79
8.4	CASE STUDIES OF REPETITION	80
8.4.1	Prime numbers	80
8.4.2	A simple grade book	80
8.4.3	Fahrenheit to Celsius converter	81
8.4.4	How many E and e are in a sentence?	82
8.5	INTERACT WITH GENAI	82

CHAPTER	9 ▪ Functions		84
9.1	WHAT ARE FUNCTIONS?		84
	9.1.1	Explanation	84
	9.1.2	Example: Bread toaster	85
	9.1.3	Practice	85
9.2	TYPES OF FUNCTIONS		86
	9.2.1	Explanation	86
9.3	DEFINE A FUNCTION		86
	9.3.1	Demonstration	86
	9.3.2	Practice	87
9.4	PARAMETERS AND ARGUMENTS		89
	9.4.1	Explanation	89
	9.4.2	Demonstration	89
	9.4.3	Practice	90
9.5	TWO PARAMETERS		92
	9.5.1	Demonstration	93
	9.5.2	Practice	93
9.6	HOW TO PASS ARGUMENTS		95
	9.6.1	Demonstration	95
	9.6.2	Practice	96
9.7	DEFAULT VALUE		96
	9.7.1	Demonstration	96
	9.7.2	Practice	97
9.8	RETURN VALUES		99
	9.8.1	Explanation	99
	9.8.2	Demonstration	99
9.9	RETURN NUMERIC VALUES		100
	9.9.1	Demonstration	100
	9.9.2	Practice	100
9.10	RETURN STR VALUES		102
	9.10.1	Demonstration	102
	9.10.2	Practice	102
9.11	RETURN BOOLEAN VALUES		102
	9.11.1	Demonstration	103
	9.11.2	Practice	103

9.12 RETURN MULTIPLE VALUES 104

    9.12.1 Demonstration 104

    9.12.2 Practice 104

9.13 INTERACT WITH GENAI 106

CHAPTER 10 ■ Advanced Functions 107

10.1 NESTED FUNCTIONS 107

    10.1.1 Explanation 107

    10.1.2 Demonstration 107

    10.1.3 Practice 108

10.2 HIERARCHICAL FUNCTIONS 110

    10.2.1 Explanation 110

    10.2.2 Demonstration 110

10.3 INTERACT WITH GENAI 112

10.4 RECURSIVE FUNCTIONS 112

    10.4.1 Explanation 112

    10.4.2 Demonstration 113

    10.4.3 Practice 113

10.5 INTERACT WITH GENAI 115

SECTION III Data Structures

CHAPTER 11 ■ List 119

11.1 WHAT IS A LIST 119

11.2 CREATE A LIST 120

    11.2.1 Demonstration 120

    11.2.2 Practice 121

11.3 HETEROGENEITY 122

    11.3.1 Demonstration 122

    11.3.2 Practice 123

    11.3.3 Test your understanding 123

11.4 ACCESS A LIST BY INDEX 124

    11.4.1 Demonstration 124

    11.4.2 Practice 125

11.5 ACCESS A LIST BY ITERATION 126

    11.5.1 Demonstration 126

    11.5.2 Practice 127

11.6 LIST MANIPULATION 128

	11.6.1	Demonstration	128
	11.6.2	Practice	129
11.7	MORE MANIPULATION OF A LIST		130
	11.7.1	Demonstration	130
	11.7.2	Practice	131
11.8	SLICE A LIST		133
	11.8.1	Demonstration	133
	11.8.2	Practice	135
11.9	LIST COMPREHENSION		136
	11.9.1	Demonstration	136
	11.9.2	Practice	138
11.10	ADVANCED LIST COMPREHENSION		139
	11.10.1	Demonstration	139
	11.10.2	Practice	140
11.11	INTERACT WITH GENAI		142
11.12	EXPLORE MORE OF LIST		142

CHAPTER 12 ▪ Tuple   143

12.1	WHAT IS A TUPLE		143
	12.1.1	Explanation	143
12.2	CREATE A TUPLE		144
	12.2.1	Demonstration	144
	12.2.2	Practice	145
12.3	HETEROGENEOUS TUPLE IN PYTHON		146
	12.3.1	Demonstration	146
	12.3.2	Practice	147
12.4	ACCESS ELEMENTS IN A TUPLE BY INDEX		147
	12.4.1	Demonstration	147
	12.4.2	Practice	149
12.5	ACCESS ELEMENTS IN A TUPLE BY ITERATION		150
	12.5.1	Demonstration	150
	12.5.2	Practice	151
12.6	SLICE A TUPLE		152
	12.6.1	Demonstration	152
	12.6.2	Practice	153
12.7	TUPLE COMPREHENSION		154
	12.7.1	Demonstration	154

	12.7.2	Practice	155
12.8	INTERACT WITH GENAI		157
12.9	EXPLORE MORE OF TUPLE		157

CHAPTER 13 ■ Set — 158

13.1	WHAT IS A SET		158
	13.1.1	Explanation	158
	13.1.2	Practice	158
13.2	CREATE A SET		159
	13.2.1	Demonstration	159
	13.2.2	Practice	160
13.3	ELEMENTS IN A SET		161
	13.3.1	Demonstration	161
	13.3.2	Practice	161
13.4	SET OPERATIONS		162
	13.4.1	Demonstration	162
	13.4.2	Practice	164
13.5	SET METHODS		165
	13.5.1	Demonstration	165
	13.5.2	Practice	166
13.6	SET COMPREHENSION		167
	13.6.1	Demonstration	167
13.7	INTERACT WITH GENAI		168
13.8	EXPLORE MORE OF SET		169

CHAPTER 14 ■ Dictionary — 170

14.1	WHAT IS A DICTIONARY		170
	14.1.1	Explanation	170
	14.1.2	Practice	171
14.2	CREATE A DICTIONARY		171
	14.2.1	Demonstration	171
	14.2.2	Practice	172
14.3	ACCESS A DICTIONARY		173
	14.3.1	Demonstration	173
	14.3.2	Practice	174
14.4	DICTIONARY METHODS		176
	14.4.1	Demonstration	176

	14.4.2	Practice	177
14.5	DICTIONARY COMPREHENSION		178
	14.5.1	Demonstration	178
	14.5.2	Practice	179
14.6	INTERACT WITH GENAI		180
14.7	EXPLORE MORE OF DICTIONARY		180

CHAPTER 15 ■ Case Studies of Data Structures   181

15.1	WARM-UP	181
15.2	DATA CREATION	182
15.3	USING LISTS	182
15.4	USING TUPLES	184
15.5	USING SETS	185
15.6	USING DICTIONARIES	185
15.7	FURTHERMORE	187
15.8	COMPLEXITY	187

SECTION IV Data Collections

CHAPTER 16 ■ Named Tuple   191

16.1	WHAT IS A NAMED TUPLE		191
	16.1.1	Explanation	191
	16.1.2	Demonstration	191
16.2	PACKAGE MANAGEMENT		192
16.3	CASE STUDY: CAR		193
16.4	INTERACT WITH GENAI		193
16.5	EXPLORE MORE OF NAMED TUPLE		194

CHAPTER 17 ■ Default Dictionary   195

17.1	WHAT IS A DEFAULT DICTIONARY		195
17.2	DEFAULT INT		197
	17.2.1	Demonstration	197
	17.2.2	Practice	197
17.3	DEFAULT LIST		198
	17.3.1	Demonstration	198
	17.3.2	Practice	199
17.4	DEFAULT SET		199
	17.4.1	Demonstration	199

17.4.2   Practice   200

17.5 CASE STUDY: HACKATHON   200

17.6 INTERACT WITH GENAI   202

17.7 EXPLORE MORE OF DEFAULT DICTIONARY   202

CHAPTER 18 ■ Counters   **203**

18.1 WHAT IS A COUNTER   203

18.2 MORE ABOUT COUNTER   204

18.2.1   Explanation   204

18.2.2   Demonstration   204

18.2.3   Practice   205

18.3 CASE STUDY: ROMEO AND JULIET   206

18.4 INTERACT WITH GENAI   207

18.5 EXPLORE MORE OF COUNTER   207

What is Next?   209

Index   211

List of Figures

1.1	A script Python example.	4
1.2	An interactive Python example.	5
1.3	Jupyter notebook example.	7
3.1	Variable x refers to 5.	20
5.1	String non-negative index.	38
5.2	String negative index.	38
5.3	String slicing with step as 1.	40
5.4	String slicing with step as 2.	41
7.1	A flow chart for optional branching.	58
7.2	A flow chart for alternative branching.	60
7.3	A flow chart for multiple branching.	63
8.1	A flow chart for condition-based repetition.	71
8.2	A flow chart for count-based repetition.	74
9.1	A function as a box.	85

List of Tables

3.1	Comparison of basic Python data types.	24
4.1	Truth table for logical operations **and**, **or**, and **not**.	32
4.2	Summary of Python operations.	34
5.1	Summary of Python string methods.	50
11.1	Summary of Python lists.	141
12.1	Summary of Python tuples.	156
13.1	Summary of Python sets.	168
14.1	Summary of Python dictionaries.	179
15.1	Summary of Python data structures.	181
15.2	Comparison of space and time complexities for Python data structures. (list, tuple, set, dictionary)	187
17.1	Summary of Python defaultdict with different default values.	202

Foreword

WHY WE NEED THIS BOOK

Start your journey into the exciting world of Python programming with this book! Designed for beginners with no prior coding experience, this book introduces Python in a refreshingly accessible way.

Forget overwhelming textbooks and long lectures, *BiteSize Python* breaks down the learning process into short, manageable lessons, each around 5–10 minutes. Whether you're busy or have trouble focusing for long periods, this approach makes it easy to fit learning Python into your daily routine.

You will learn essential Python concepts effortlessly through engaging lessons, practice labs, and real-world examples. From grasping basic syntax to writing your own programs, this book gives you the skills and confidence to become a capable Python programmer.

What makes *BiteSize Python* unique is its adaptability to your learning style. Whether you enjoy hands-on practice, self-reflection exercises, reviewing solutions, or interacting with generative AI, this book has something for everyone.

Discover the joy of learning Python at your own pace and unlock endless possibilities in the programming world. With this book, start your journey toward empowerment, efficiency, and practical skills that will quickly transform you from a beginner to a confident Python programmer.

Preface

WHY THIS BOOK IS DIFFERENT

While there are many books, websites, and online courses about the topic, we differentiate our book in multiple ways:

- BiteSize Approach: Breaks down Python programming into easily digestible lessons of less than 5 minutes each.

- Beginner-Friendly: Designed for absolute beginners with no prior programming experience.

- Practical Learning: Offers hands-on practice labs and real-world examples to reinforce learning.

- Time-Efficient: Ideal for individuals with busy schedules or limited time for studying.

- Comprehensive Coverage: Covers essential Python concepts and skills necessary for writing basic programs.

- Interactive Learning: Includes self-reflection exercises and solutions review to enhance understanding and retention.

SPECIFIC AIMS

As an introduction to Python, this book allows readers to take a slow and steady approach to understanding Python code, explaining concepts, connecting programming with real-life examples, writing Python programs, and completing case studies. The aims of this book are as follows:

- Give a simple and easy-to-understand introduction to Python programming for people who are complete beginners.

- Break down the learning process into bite-sized lessons to accommodate readers' limited time and attention spans.

- Help readers understand Python code and develop the skills to write their own programs.

- Provide a range of learning formats, including concept overviews, practice labs, and self-reflection exercises, to fit different learning styles.

- Showcase many interesting case studies and provide readers with a solid understanding of how to apply the knowledge to our real world.

HOW TO USE THIS BOOK

This book is made to give you a rich and engaging learning experience. Our method focuses on *BiteSize* learning, making hard topics easy by breaking them down into simple, understandable parts:

- Each lesson begins with a clear and short *introduction* to the topic. This gives you a strong base to start from and gets you ready for deeper learning.

- After the introduction, you will see *coding demonstrations* that show the ideas discussed. These examples are simple and useful, helping you really understand the concepts.

- After the introduction and demo, it's time to practice! The *practice* tasks come in different difficulty levels, so you can test your knowledge and grow your confidence. Make sure you try hard before checking the solutions!

- To help you learn better, we suggest using *Generative AI* tools like ChatGPT for feedback, practice exercises, code reviews, and finding advanced topics. These prompts can help you see where to improve, review main ideas, and think about your progress. We actually adopted some of the prompts that are created by AI in this book! Generative AI as a tool is great, but only we should use it wisely.

- Apply Python to make a difference! *Case studies* combine all the small ideas to show how you can use them to solve real-world problems.

- Most coding demos, practice tasks, and case studies come with *Jupyter Notebooks*. This format allows you to look at, change, and run the code, giving you a hands-on experience that makes learning more fun.

We believe this book will guide you step by step to learn Python and use it confidently in real life. No matter whether you are new to coding or just want to improve your Python skills, this book will help you reach your learning goals through these little fun *Bites*!

INTERACT WITH AI

To get the most out of your interaction with a generative AI tool like ChatGPT, always begin your conversation with the following prompt:

"You are an expert in Python programming. Act as a tutor helping a student who is learning Python programming."

This prompt sets the tone for the conversation and ensures the AI will provide helpful and detailed guidance tailored to your learning. Here are some general suggestions and prompts for effective interaction:

- Can you explain how [concept] works?
- What's the difference between [concept 1] and [concept 2]?
- Can you provide an example of a function that does [specific task]?
- Show me how to use a [specific structure or method] to achieve [goal].
- I don't understand why [specific method] isn't working. Can you help me troubleshoot it?
- My code: "[Your Python Code]" is not running. What is wrong? Can you correct it?
- Review my code: "[Your Python Code]." Can you improve my code to make it more professional?
- Can you explain why [specific aspect] works this way?

In each Interact with GenAI section, we prepared specific suggestions and prompts for the specific topic as well. We hope you can utilize generative AI as a great tool to enhance and assist your learning.

ACKNOWLEDGEMENT

The author has utilized various Generative AI models, including ChatGPT (4o-mini), Gemini (2.0), Claude(3.5 Haiku), Gemma(1.1:7b, 2:9b), Llama (3.1:8b, 3.2:3b), and Apple Intelligence (Beta), to improve the language, proofread code comments, and come up with some ideas for the "Interact with GenAI" section. All the text generated by generative AI has been carefully reviewed and revised to meet academic standards.

I would also like to acknowledge the reviewers, editors, and publishers for making the book happen.

Author Bios

Dr. Di Wu is an Assistant Professor of Finance, Information Systems, and Economics department of Business School, Lehman College. He obtained a Ph.D. in Computer Science from the Graduate Center, CUNY. Dr. Wu's research interests are 1) Temporal extensions to RDF and semantic web, 2) Applied Data Science, and 3) Experiential Learning and Pedagogy in business education. Dr. Wu developed and taught courses including Strategic Management, Databases, Business Statistics, Management Decision Making, Programming Languages (C++, Java, and Python), Data Structures and Algorithms, Data Mining, Big Data, and Machine Learning.

I

Python Fundamentals

SECTION I: PYTHON FUNDAMENTALS introduces the essential concepts of Python, a versatile and widely used programming language known for its simplicity and readability. You will learn about Python's strengths, including why it has become the language of choice for many developers. This section will explain the difference between script-based and interactive Python environments, highlighting the benefits of using local and cloud-based Jupyter notebooks for coding. Key foundational elements such as the `print()` and `input()` functions will be covered, along with variables, operations, and string manipulation using built-in methods.

By the end of this section, you will be able to:

- Understand Python's core principles and advantages as a programming language.

- Differentiate between script-based and interactive Python environments, and effectively use Jupyter Notebooks.

- Use `print()` and `input()` to interact with users and display the output.

- Understand Python's variable and dynamic typing.

- Operate with the basic data types, including `int`, `float`, `str`, and `bool`.

- Perform operations with variables and manipulate strings using Python's built-in methods.

## CHAPTER 1

Introduction to Python

WELCOME to the world of Python! You might have heard of this magical language before, maybe in a school assignment, a software manual, or a code snippet your colleague sent you. You know it's important for the ever-changing tech world. Yes, you are absolutely right! Even if you don't need to use it every day, learning Python will be a unique experience and a smart investment of your time. It'll teach you how computers think and work, how programs and classes are designed, and how sophisticated neutrons are built and connected to form the foundation of artificial intelligence. This chapter will answer some basic questions about Python, like what it is, why it's so popular, what it looks like, where to develop and run it, what the Jupyter Notebook is, where to write the code, etc. Let's get started!

1.1 WHAT IS PYTHON?

Python is a high-level, interpreted programming language that's known for being easy to learn and use, making it a popular choice for beginners. It was created by Guido van Rossum, a Dutch programmer, and first released in 1991. The language is named after the British comedy group Monty Python's Flying Circus, not after the snake, despite the reptilian logo! Guido just thought the snake design would make for a cool logo.

Over the years, Python has seen many updates and improvements. Python 2.0 came out in 2000, introducing a garbage collector and a new memory management system. For a long time, Python 2.x was widely used, but it had some drawbacks, like limited support for Unicode. As of now, Python 2.x is no longer supported or maintained, so we'll focus on Python 3.x in this book. Python 3.0, released in 2008, tackled the limitations of Python 2.x and added many new features.

The latest version, Python 3.13, was released on October 7, 2024. Python 3.x is fully Unicode-compatible, offers better support for parallel processing, and includes a host of new modules and libraries for tasks like data analysis, web development, and more.

It's also the preferred version for many popular frameworks and libraries, including Django, Flask, NumPy, and pandas.

1.2 WHY PYTHON?

Python's popularity comes from its ease of use, versatility, and strong community support.

Python is known for being simple and easy to read. It has a small set of keywords and a clean structure, making it easy for beginners to learn and understand. The syntax is designed to be straightforward, so developers can focus on the logic of their code rather than getting caught up in complex syntax. Python also has many libraries and frameworks that simplify tasks like data analysis and web development.

Python is a general-purpose language, meaning it can be used for a wide variety of tasks, including web development, data analysis, artificial intelligence (AI), machine learning, and automation. Its versatility makes it a popular choice for different types of projects, and its large developer community offers many libraries and frameworks to help with almost any task.

Python has a big, active community of developers who create libraries, frameworks, and tools for various tasks. This strong community support provides plenty of resources for learning and troubleshooting, making it easy to find help. Python's community-driven development also ensures that the language keeps evolving to meet users' needs.

Python works on multiple operating systems, like Windows, macOS, and Linux. It is also open-source, meaning it is free to use, share, and modify. This open-source nature has led to a large community of developers who contribute to Python's development, ensuring it remains a high-quality and continually improving language.

1.3 SCRIPT VERSUS INTERACTIVE PYTHON

When working with Python, you have two main options for your environment: script Python and interactive Python. Script Python involves writing code in a text editor or integrated development environment (IDE) and running it as a script, while interactive Python allows you to execute code line by line and see the results immediately.

Script Python is ideal for tasks that require automation, such as data processing, web scraping, or system administration. You write a script, save it, and run it as needed. Script Python is great for tasks that require repetition or need to be run in the background (Figure 1.1).

```
hello.py
print('Hello, world!') # Display a message
```

Figure 1.1 A script Python example.

Interactive Python, on the other hand, is perfect for data science, scientific computing, and exploratory data analysis. With interactive Python, you can execute code line by line, see the results, and adjust your code accordingly. This iterative process allows you to explore data, test hypotheses, and visualize results in real time (Figure 1.2).

ˇ Demonstration

```
[ ]  print('Hello, world!') # display a message
⊐⊤  Hello, world!
```

Figure 1.2 An interactive Python example.

1.4 WHY INTERACTIVE PYTHON?

Interactive Python is particularly well-suited for data science for the following reasons:

- It enables you to load data, manipulate it, and visualize it in real time. This allows you to quickly understand the structure and patterns in your data, identify missing or incorrect values, and perform exploratory data analysis.

- It allows you to write and test machine learning models iteratively. You can try out different algorithms, fine-tune hyperparameters, and evaluate model performance in real time, enabling you to quickly refine your models and achieve better results.

- It provides access to a wide range of statistical libraries and tools, such as Pandas, NumPy, and Scikit-learn. You can perform statistical analysis, data transformation, and feature engineering in an interactive environment, making it easier to understand and prepare your data for modeling.

- It enables you to create interactive visualizations and dashboards using libraries like Matplotlib, Seaborn, and Plotly. This allows you to present your findings in a clear and compelling way, enabling stakeholders to explore and understand the insights you've uncovered.

- Its interactive nature allows you to write and test code quickly, enabling you to debug your code in a fast and iterative manner. This reduces the time and effort required to develop and refine your data science projects.

- Its environments like Jupyter Notebook enable collaboration and sharing of code, data, and results. This facilitates teamwork and knowledge sharing among data scientists, engineers, and other stakeholders.

1.5 JUPYTER

For our book, we'll be using JupyterLab and Jupyter Notebooks as our interactive Python environment. Jupyter Notebooks blend explanations, images and rich media, codes, and outputs in one document. It's an ideal platform for data science, scientific computing, and education and is widely used in industry, academia, and research. JupyterLab is a web-based user interface to create and play with Jupyter Notebooks.

Jupyter Notebook's interactive cells allow you to execute code line by line, seeing the results of each cell in real time. This enables you to explore data, test hypotheses, and visualize results in an iterative and dynamic manner. You can write code in Python, R, Julia, or other languages and execute it in the browser or on a remote server.

Jupyter Notebooks support a wide range of media, including images, videos, interactive visualizations, and equations. You can embed these media elements directly into your notebooks, making it easy to create engaging and interactive documents. This is particularly useful for data visualization, where you can create interactive plots and charts that allow users to explore data in real time.

Jupyter Notebooks enable real-time collaboration and sharing of documents. You can share notebooks with others and work together on a single document in real time. This facilitates teamwork and knowledge sharing among data scientists, engineers, and other stakeholders. You can also use Jupyter Notebook's built-in commenting and discussion features to communicate with collaborators and stakeholders.

Jupyter Notebooks have access to a wide range of libraries and tools, including popular data science libraries like Pandas, NumPy, and Scikit-learn. You can also install additional libraries and tools, such as Matplotlib, Seaborn, and Plotly, to extend the functionality of your notebooks. This enables you to perform a wide range of data science tasks, from data cleaning and visualization to machine learning and deep learning.

Jupyter Notebooks provide robust security and scalability features, making them suitable for use in production environments. You can secure your notebooks with passwords, tokens, or other authentication methods and scale your notebooks to handle large datasets and high traffic. This enables you to deploy your notebooks in a variety of environments, from local machines to cloud-based servers.

Jupyter Notebook files have a `.ipynb` extension and contain a JavaScript Object Notation structure that represents the notebook's contents. These files can be opened and edited in Jupyter Notebook and can also be shared and collaborated on with others. The `.ipynb` file format allows for a flexible and dynamic document that can contain a mix of text, code, equations, images, and interactive visualizations.

One of the key features of Jupyter Notebooks is the ability to combine markdown text, code cells, and output cells in a single document. This allows you to create a narrative document that explains your code, shows the output of your code, and provides a clear and concise explanation of your results.

1. Markdown cells allow you to write text in a simple and readable format, using markdown syntax to format headings, bold text, italics, and links. You can use markdown cells to provide explanations, introductions, and summaries, as well as to add context to your code and output.
2. Code cells allow you to write and execute code in a variety of programming languages, including Python, R, Julia, and MATLAB. You can use code cells to perform data analysis, machine learning, and visualization, as well as to create interactive plots and charts.
3. Output cells display the results of your code, including text, images, and interactive visualizations. You can use output cells to show the output of your code and to create reports and dashboards that summarize your findings.

By combining markdown, code, and output cells, you can create a clear and concise narrative document that explains your code, shows the output of your code, and provides a summary of your results. This is particularly useful for data science and scientific computing, where you need to document your methods, results, and conclusions in a clear and transparent way (Figure 1.3).

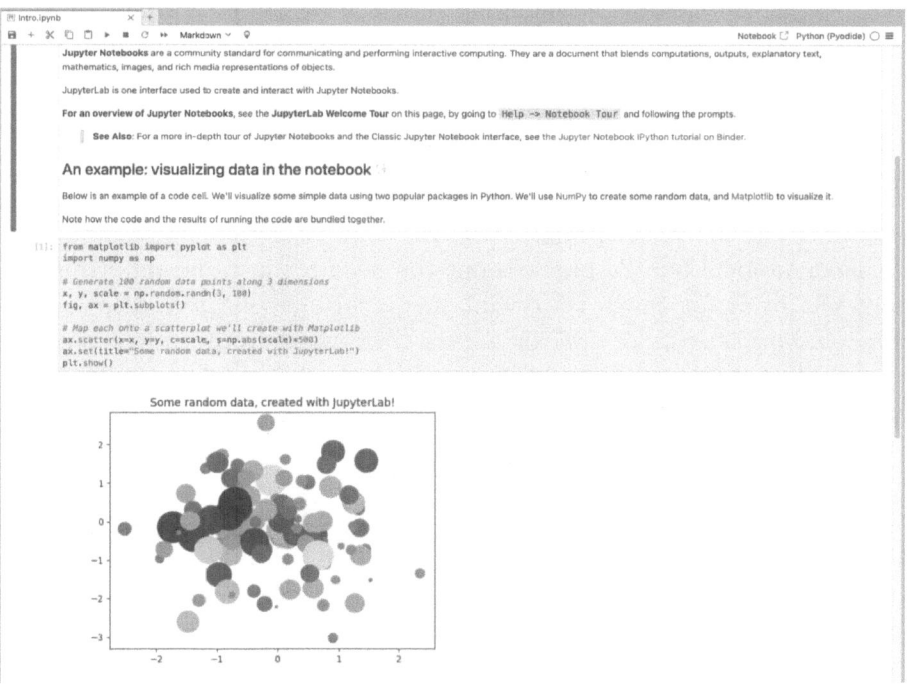

Figure 1.3 Jupyter notebook example.

1.6 LOCAL OR CLOUD

When it comes to using Jupyter Notebooks for Python development, you have two main options: local installation or cloud services. Local installation involves downloading and installing Jupyter Notebooks on your own computer, giving you full control over the environment and the ability to work offline. However, this requires technical expertise and can be time-consuming to set up. On the other hand, cloud services like Google Colaboratory (Google Colab), Anaconda Online, and others offer a hassle-free and convenient alternative. With cloud services, you can access Jupyter Notebooks from anywhere, without the need for installation or maintenance. You can focus on writing code and collaborating with others, while the cloud service handles the technical details.

Anaconda local bundle is a self-contained package that includes the Anaconda distribution, Jupyter Notebooks, and other popular data science tools. By installing it on your local machine, you have complete control over the environment and can work offline. This is ideal for those who require a high level of customization, security, and offline access. Additionally, local installation allows for faster performance and responsiveness, making it suitable for large-scale data processing and computation. However, it requires technical expertise to set up and maintain and can be resource-intensive.

Google Colab is a popular cloud service that offers Jupyter Notebooks for free, with no setup required. You can access it from anywhere, and it comes with many popular libraries pre-installed, including TensorFlow and PyTorch. Additionally, Google Colab offers features like real-time collaboration, version control, and easy sharing of notebooks. Whether you're a student, researcher, or professional, cloud services offer a convenient and powerful way to use Jupyter Notebook for Python development.

Anaconda Online is another cloud-based platform that offers a managed environment for data science and machine learning. It provides access to the same tools and libraries as the Anaconda local bundle but without the need for installation or maintenance. This makes it ideal for those who want to quickly get started with data science projects, collaborate with others, or access their work from anywhere. Anaconda Online also offers features like real-time collaboration, version control, and easy sharing of notebooks.

1.7 LEARNING PYTHON

We adopt the experiential learning pedagogy and Bite-Size strategy to break a hard topic down into fun pieces. This approach enables learners to engage with Python programming in a hands-on, iterative, and incremental manner. By using these methods, learners can gain a better understanding of Python, improve their problem-solving skills, and build a growth mindset.

To learn Python effectively, it is essential to understand the logic behind the syntax. Python's syntax is designed to be intuitive and concise, but it is crucial to grasp the underlying principles to write efficient and readable code.

Practice is key to learning Python. Start with simple programs and gradually move on to more complex case studies, even projects. The more you code, the more comfortable you'll become with Python's syntax, and the better you'll understand how to apply it to real-world problems.

To make learning Python more engaging and relevant, connect the concepts you learn to real-world examples. Think about how Python can be used to solve problems in your own life or in your desired field. By connecting Python to real-world scenarios, you'll stay motivated and see the practical value of what you are learning.

Finally, utilize the power of Generative AI to enhance your learning journey. Use AI-powered tools to generate explanations, examples, and practice exercises specific to your unique needs. With generative AI, you can get personalized feedback, correct your mistakes, and reinforce your understanding of Python concepts.

## CHAPTER 2

Input and Output

N ow , you have a general idea about Python. It's time for you to write your first Python program. In this chapter, you will learn how to display messages on the screen using the `print()` function and how to obtain information from users using the `input()` function. Combining `print()` and `input()` enables you to write programs that can interact with users!

Are you ready? Let's get started!

2.1 HELLO, WORLD!

2.1.1 Demonstration

```python
print('Hello, world!') # display a message
```

```
Hello, world!
```

The `print()` function is a built-in Python function that outputs text to the screen. It's a fundamental function in Python, and you'll use it frequently to display output, debug your code, and provide feedback to users. We will learn functions in detail in later chapters.

The string `'Hello, world!'` is a sequence of characters enclosed in a pair of single quotation marks (`'`). In Python, strings can be enclosed in either single quotation marks or double quotation marks (`""`). The string `'Hello, world!'` is a literal string, meaning it's a fixed sequence of characters that doesn't change. We will learn the data types and strings in detail in later chapters.

The syntax for the `print()` function is `print(value)`, where value is the text or value you want to output. In this case, the value is the string `'Hello, world!'`.

The `# display a message` is an in-line comment. Everything to the right of the `#` symbol will be ignored by the Python interpreter, allowing you to add notes and explanations to your code without affecting its functionality. In-line comments are a

DOI: 10.1201/9781003527725-2

great way to add quick notes and reminders to your code and can help make your code more readable and understandable.

2.1.2 Practice

Note: Before looking at the solutions provided in this book for the practice tasks, try your best to complete the tasks on your own. Struggling with the tasks actually will help you understand the concepts better. Additionally, keep in mind that our solutions are not the only correct ones. Your approach might be different but also valid.

Task: Change the value in the `print()` in the demonstration to be `'Hello, Python!'` and print it out.

```
print('Hello, Python!')
```

Hello, Python!

Task: Change the value in the `print()` in the demonstration to be `'Hello, {your name}!'` and print it out. Note that the `{your name}` is a place holder and you should replace it with your name. For example, `Neo`.

```
print('Hello, Neo!')
```

Hello, Neo!

2.2 SINGLE OR DOUBLE

2.2.1 Explanation

In Python, you can use either single quotation mark (`'`) or double quotation mark (`"`) to define a string. This means that `'Hello, world!'` and `"Hello, world!"` are equivalent and will produce the same output.

Python allows both single and double quotations to make it easier to define strings that contain quotations. For example, if you want to define a string that contains a single quotation, you can use double quotation: `"It's a beautiful day!"`. Similarly, if you want to define a string that contains a double quotation, you can use single quotation: `'He said, "Hello, world!"'`.

While Python allows both single and double quotations, it's generally recommended to use single quotes for defining strings. This is because single quotes are more commonly used in Python and make the code more readable. Additionally, single quotes are less prone to errors, as they don't require escaping when defining strings that contain double quotes.

Escaping allows you to include special characters in your strings by prefixing them with a backslash (\). This tells Python to treat the next character as a literal character, rather than its special meaning.

2.2.2 Demonstration

```
# Same output as single quotations
print("Hello, world!")
```

Hello, world!

```
# Raise error because the string contains a single quotation
print('I'm fine.')
```

```
  File "<ipython-input-1-c130f7fb8291>", line 2
    print('I'm fine.')
              ^
```

SyntaxError: unterminated string literal (detected at line 2)

```
# Escaping the quotation to avoid conflict
print('I\'m fine.')
```

I'm fine.

```
# Use double quotations to avoid conflict
print("I'm fine.")
```

I'm fine.

```
# Raise error because the string contains a double quotation
print("He said "No!"")
```

```
  File "<ipython-input-8-d24e08d6fbf5>", line 2
    print("He said "No!"")
                ^
```

SyntaxError: invalid syntax. Perhaps you forgot a comma?

```
# Escaping the quotation to avoid conflict
print("He said \"No!\"")
```

He said "No!"

```
# Use single quotations to avoid conflict
print('He said "No!"')
```

He said "No!"

2.2.3 Practice

Task: Print a string 'Don't worry, be happy!' using double quotations

```
print("Don't worry, be happy!")
```

Don't worry, be happy!

Task: Print a string 'Don't worry, be happy!' using escape

```
print('Don\'t worry, be happy!')
```

Don't worry, be happy!

Task: Print a string `'"Yes! I promise!"'` using single quotations

```
print('"Yes! I promise!"')
```

"Yes! I promise!"

Task: Print a string `'"Yes! I promise!"'` using escape

```
print("\"Yes! I promise!\"")
```

"Yes! I promise!"

2.3 TRIPLE QUOTATIONS

2.3.1 Explanation

Python also allows triple quotations (`"""` or `'''`) to define multiline strings. Triple quotations are used to define strings that span multiple lines, and they preserve the newline characters. Triple quotations are useful when you need to define a long string that contains multiple lines of text. They are also useful when you need to define a string that contains quotes, as you don't need to escape the quotations.

Python also uses triple quotations (`"""` or `'''`) to define multiline comments. Multiline comments are used to document your code and explain what it does. They can span multiple lines and are ignored by the Python interpreter. To define a multiline comment, you simply enclose your text in triple quotations.

```
# Same output as single and double quotations
print('''Hello, world!''')
```

Hello, world!

```
# Worry-free for strings with single or double quotations
print('''She said: "We're good!"''')
```

She said: "We're good!"

```
# Multi-line strings
print('''This is a
multiline
string
example''')
```

This is a
multiline
string
example

```
'''This is a
multiline
string
comments'''
print('Hello, world!')
```

Hello, world!

2.3.2 Practice

Task: print the poem below using one `print()`

```
This
is
a
poem
```

```python
print('''This
is
a
poem
''')
```

```
This
is
a
poem
```

Task: print the paragraph below using one `print()`

```
This is a multi-line
documentary. It consists
several sentences and
might be pages long.
```

```python
print('''This is a multi-line
documentary. It consists
several sentences and
might be pages long.
''')
```

```
This is a multi-line
documentary. It consists
several sentences and
might be pages long.
```

Task: print the dialog below using one `print()`

```
"How are you?"
"I'm fine."
"It's a great day!"
```

```python
print('''"How are you?"
"I'm fine."
"It's a great day!"''')
```

```
"How are you?"
"I'm fine."
"It's a great day!"
```

2.4   PRINT MULTIPLE VALUES

2.4.1   Demonstration

In Python, the `print()` function is used to output text or values to the screen. But what if you want to print multiple values at once? That's where the comma (`,`) comes in! When you separate values with a comma inside the `print()` function, Python will output each value separated by a space `' '`. This makes it easy to print multiple values in a single statement.

```python
# Observe the differences between the two commas below
print('Hello,', 'world!')
```

```
Hello, world!
```

In the above example, the first comma is within `' '` thus, it is part of the string and the second comma is used to separate the two values.

2.4.2   Practice

Task: Use `print()` to print two values `'Python'` and `'3.12'` out.

```python
print('Python', '3.12')
```

```
Python 3.12
```

Task: Use `print()` to print four values `'What'`, `'a'`, `'wonderful'`, and `'world!'` out.

```python
print('What', 'a', 'wonderful', 'world!')
```

```
What a wonderful world!
```

2.5   INTERACT WITH GENAI

To get the most out of your interaction with a generative AI tool like ChatGPT, always begin your conversation with the following prompt:

"You are an expert in Python programming. Act as a tutor helping a student who is learning Python programming."

This prompt sets the tone for the conversation and ensures the AI will provide helpful and detailed guidance tailored to your learning. Here are some general suggestions and prompts for effective interaction:

- Can you explain how [concept] works?
- What's the difference between [concept 1] and [concept 2]?
- Can you provide an example of a function that does [specific task]?
- Show me how to use a [specific structure or method] to achieve [goal].
- I don't understand why [specific method] isn't working. Can you help me troubleshoot it?

- My code: "[Your Python Code]" is not running. What is wrong? Can you correct it?
- Review my code: "[Your Python Code]". Can you improve my code to make it more professional?
- Can you explain why [specific aspect] works this way?

We also prepared specific suggestions and prompts for `print` as well.

- What is the purpose of the `print()` function in Python?
- How does the `print()` function display output in Python?
- What types of data can be passed to the `print()` function in Python?
- Show how to print a simple string using the `print()` function.
- Demonstrate printing multiple variables in one line with a space separator.
- What should you do if `print()` isn't displaying the expected output?
- How can you fix issues with extra spaces between printed values when using `print()`?

We hope you can utilize generative AI as a great tool to enhance and assist your learning.

2.6 GET INPUTS

We can use the `print()` function to show a message on the screen. But what if we want to get the message our users give us? That's where the `input()` function comes in. Let's observe the demonstration.

2.6.1 Demonstration

```
input('What is your name?') # display a prompt
```

What is your name?Neo

```
{"type":"string"}
```

The `input()` function is a built-in Python function that allows your program to get user input. Its purpose is to read input from the user and return it as a string.

The string `'What is your name?'` is an argument that the `input()` function takes in. The argument is displayed as a prompt to the user. This prompt helps guide the user on what input is expected.

The syntax for the `input()` function is `input(value)`, where value is the instruction text as the prompt you want to show to the user. In this case, the value is the string `'What is your name?'`.

2.6.2 Practice

Task: Display a prompt `'Where do you live?'` and get it from the user

```
input('Where do you live?')
```

Task: Display a prompt `'How do you feel so far? Enter 1 for Good; 2 for very good: '` and get it from the user

```
input('How do you feel so far? Enter 1 for Good; 2 for very good.')
```

Task: Display a prompt `'Are you ready to learn more? Enter Yes or No: '` and get it from the user

```
input('Are you ready to learn more? Enter Yes or No.')
```

2.7 COMBINE `PRINT()` AND `INPUT()`

2.7.1 Explanation

You may have noticed that when you use the `input()` function, the value the user enters is displayed as a string with single quotations. This is because the `input()` function always returns a string. Even if the user enters a number, it will be returned as a string.

Now, let's combine the `input()` function with the `print()` function. Since the value returned by the `input()` function is a string, we can use it as an argument to the `print()` function to display the user's input.

2.7.2 Demonstration

```
print('Hello,', input('What is your name? '), '!')
```

```
What is your name? Neo
Hello, Neo !
```

```
print('Today is', input('What weekday is today? '))
```

```
What weekday is today? Friday
Today is Friday
```

```
print(input('What is your first name? '),
      input('What is your last name?'),
      'is awesome!')
```

```
What is your first name? Thomas
What is your last name?Anderson
Thomas Anderson is awesome!
```

2.7.3 Practice

Task: Display a prompt `'What date is today? yyyymmdd: '` to get value from the user, then print the value on the screen.

```
print(input('What date is today? yyyymmdd: '))
```

```
What date is today? yyyymmdd: 20240501
20240501
```

Task: Display a prompt `'How old are you? '` to get value from the user, then print the value on the screen.

```
print(input('How old are you? '))
```

```
How old are you? 18
18
```

Task: Display a prompt `'Which number is your lucky number? '` to get value from the user, then print the value and a string `'is a magic number!'` on the screen.

```
print(input('Which number is your lucky number? '), 'is a magic number!')
```

```
Which number is your lucky number? 9
9 is a magic number!
```

2.8   INTERACT WITH GENAI

Here are some questions and prompts you can interact with generative AI tools, including ChatGPT.

- What is the purpose of the `input()` function in Python?
- How does the `input()` function capture user input in Python?
- What data type does the `input()` function return by default?
- How can you use the `input()` function to prompt the user with a custom message?
- What happens if the user enters an invalid value when using `input()`?
- Show how to capture the user's name using the `input()` function.
- Demonstrate how to capture and display the user's age using `input()`.
- Use `input()` to prompt the user to enter their favorite color and print a response based on their choice.
- What happens if the user accidentally presses Enter without entering anything when using `input()`?

## CHAPTER 3

Variables

How do you feel about Python so far? You can obtain information from users and display them on the screen! Python is not that hard, right? Let's add some flavors to make it more useful now. In this chapter, we are going to learn the concept of variables, including how to define them and use them, and the dynamic typing in Python. We will also learn data types, so we can represent data in terms of built-in `int`, `float`, `str`, and `bool` values. Are you ready? Let's get started!

3.1 WHAT ARE VARIABLES

3.1.1 Explanation

Variables are used to store and reference values in a program. Without variables, we would have to repeat code or hardcode values, making our programs inflexible and difficult to maintain. Variables allow us to store a value once and use it multiple times, making our code more efficient and easier to read.

In Python, variables work as references, meaning they point to the location in memory where the actual value is stored. This means that when we assign a new value to a variable, we are updating the reference to point to the new value, rather than changing the original value. This concept of references is key to understanding how variables work in Python, and it allows for powerful and flexible programming. With variables, we can write more dynamic and interactive programs that can adapt to changing conditions and user input. For example:

```
x = 5
```

Now, we can use `x` in any and many places, and the value of `x` is 5. If we need to update the value, just assign a new value to `x`, and all places `x` was used, will be updated (Figure 3.1).

DOI: 10.1201/9781003527725-3

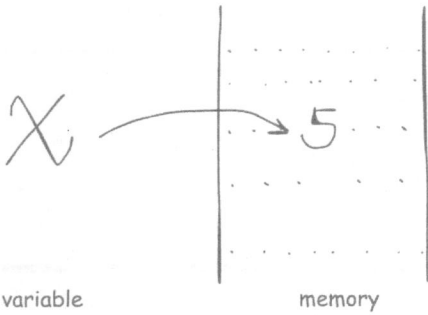

variable   memory

Figure 3.1 Variable x refers to 5.

3.1.2 Practice

Task: Think about in your real life, what kind of references we may use. For example:

```
input('Where do you live?')
```

Yes. When we mention a place in a conversation, we are referencing the physical location! Do you have some other examples?

3.2 NAMING RULES

3.2.1 Explanation

There are two levels of naming rules. The minimal level has hard rules following the syntax. You must satisfy the syntax rules of naming variables; otherwise, you'll get errors. The other level has soft rules following the convention. It is recommended to satisfy the convention rules so you can write professional programs.

Syntax rules are:

- Variable names must start with a letter (a-z or A-Z) or an underscore (_).
- Variable names can only contain letters (a-z or A-Z), digits (0-9), and underscores (_).
- Variable names are case-sensitive (e.g., name and Name are treated as different variables).
- Variable names cannot be reserved keywords (e.g., if, else, while, etc.).

Convention rules are:

- Variable names should be descriptive and indicate the purpose of the variable.
- Variable names should be concise, but not so short that they are unclear.
- Variable names should use lowercase letters and underscores to separate words (e.g., first_name instead of FirstName).
- Variable names should avoid using abbreviations or acronyms unless they are widely recognized (e.g., id for identifier).

- Variable names should not start with an underscore (_) (even if it's allowed by the syntax rules) unless you understand the special usage of this form.

By following these syntax rules and convention rules, you can write clear, readable, and maintainable code that makes it easy for others (and yourself) to understand what your variables represent.

3.2.2 Practice

Task: In following variable names, mark them with

1. Error (break synatx rules)
2. Not good (break convention rules)
3. Good (following all rules)

```
# application_id: GOOD
# b: NOT GOOD
# Cat: NOT GOOD
# 4square: ERROR
# five!: ERROR
# six_dice: GOOD
# _seven_day: NOT GOOD
# eight_9:NOT ERROR -- NOT GOOD
# Ten_points: NOT GOOD
# lIama3: NOT GOOD
# bubble_O0o: NOT GOOD
# gj: NOT GOOD
```

3.3 DATA TYPES

3.3.1 Explanation

In Python, a variable can refer to any type of value. The built-in data types include:

- Integers `int`: e.g., 1, 2, 3, -3
- Floats `float`: e.g., 3.14, -0.5
- Strings `str`: e.g., "hello", 'hello')
- Booleans `bool`: e.g., `True`, `False`

In Python, the data type of a variable is determined by the data type of the value it refers to. This means that the data type of a variable is not fixed or declared beforehand, but rather is inferred from the value that the variable is referring to in real time. For example, if you assign an integer value to a variable, the variable will be considered an integer type; if you then assign a string value to that variable, the variable will be considered a string type, and so on. This is known as dynamic typing, and it allows for flexibility in programming, as a variable can change its data type during runtime if a different type of value is assigned to it. This is different from statically typed languages, where the data type of a variable is fixed.

3.3.2 Practice

For all tasks below, use `print()` and `type()` to check the value is correctly assigned and the data type is correct. For example: `print('x:', x, type(x))`. Note that the `type()` will return the data type of values or variables.

Task: assign x with an int 5.

```
# Assign the value 5 to the variable x
x = 5

# Print the value of x, followed by its data type
print('x:', x, type(x))
```

x: 5 <class 'int'>

Task: assign int_x with x.

```
int_x = x
print('x:', x, type(x))
print('int_x:', int_x, type(int_x))
```

x: 5 <class 'int'>
int_x: 5 <class 'int'>

Task: assign x with a float 5.0.

```
x = 5.0
print('x:', x, type(x))
```

x: 5.0 <class 'float'>

Task: assign float_x with x.

```
float_x = x
print('x:', x, type(x))
print('float_x:', float_x, type(float_x))
```

x: 5.0 <class 'float'>
float_x: 5.0 <class 'float'>

Task: assign x with a str '5'.

```
x = '5'
print('x:', x, type(x))
```

x: 5 <class 'str'>

Task: assign str1_x with x.

```
str1_x = x
print('x:', x, type(x))
print('str1_x:', str1_x, type(str1_x))
```

x: 5 <class 'str'>
str1_x: 5 <class 'str'>

Task: assign x with a str '5.0'.

```
x = '5.0'
print('x:', x, type(x))
```

x: 5.0 <class 'str'>

Task: assign str2_x with x.

```
str2_x = x
print('x:', x, type(x))
print('str2_x:', str2_x, type(str2_x))
```

x: 5.0 <class 'str'>
str2_x: 5.0 <class 'str'>

Task: Use print() and type() to check all the variables you created so far, x, int_x, float_x, str1_x, str2_x for their values and data types.

```
print('x:', x, type(x))
print('int_x:', int_x, type(int_x))
print('float_x:', float_x, type(float_x))
print('str1_x:', str1_x, type(str1_x))
print('str2_x:', str2_x, type(str2_x))
```

x: 5.0 <class 'str'>
int_x: 5 <class 'int'>
float_x: 5.0 <class 'float'>
str1_x: 5 <class 'str'>
str2_x: 5.0 <class 'str'>

3.4 DATA TYPES CONVERT

3.4.1 Explanation

In Python, you can convert a value from one data type to another using various conversion functions. This is useful when you need to work with values of different types or when you need to ensure a value is in a specific format.

3.4.2 Demonstration

```
x = 5 # x is an int
print(str(x), type(str(x)))
```

5 <class 'str'>

```
x = 5 # x is an int
print(float(x), type(float(x)))
```

5.0 <class 'float'>

```
x = 5.0 # x is a float
print(int(x), type(int(x)))
```

5 <class 'int'>

```
x = 5.5 # x is a float
print(int(x), type(int(x)))
```

```
5 <class 'int'>
```

```
x = '5' # x is a str
print(int(x), type(int(x)))
```

```
5 <class 'int'>
```

```
x = '5.5' # x is a str
print(float(x), type(float(x)))
```

```
5.5 <class 'float'>
```

Be careful if you convert values between different data types. Sometimes you may encounter errors, for example, try to convert a string literal ('a') to a float or ('5.5') to an integer. Sometimes you may have data loss, for example, try to convert '5.5' to an `int`, which returns the floor value (5) instead of the actual value (6).

Let's summarize the data types and compare them in Table 3.1.

Table 3.1 Comparison of basic Python data types.

	int	float	str	bool
Definition	Integers	Floating-point numbers	Sequence of characters	Boolean values
Example	42	3.14	"hello"	True, False
Constructor	int()	float()	str()	bool()
Mutability	Immutable	Immutable	Immutable	Immutable
Applications	Counting, indexing	Measurements, calculations, scientific data	Text, data representation	Condition, logic control
Pros	Precise for discrete values, efficient	Handles large ranges and decimals	Rich library of string methods, flexible	Simple and intuitive for logic-based code
Cons	Cannot handle decimals, may overflow	Precision for very large or small numbers	Memory-intensive for large strings	Limited values

3.4.3 Practice

For all tasks below, use print() and type() to check the value is correctly assigned, and the data type is correct. For example `print('x:', x, type(x))`

Task: convert a str '0' to int

```
x = int('0')
print('x:', x, type(x))
```

```
x: 0 <class 'int'>
```

Task: convert a float 0.1 to int

```
x = int(0.1)
print('x:', x, type(x))
```

x: 0 <class 'int'>

Task: convert a str '0' to float

```
x = float('0')
print('x:', x, type(x))
```

x: 0.0 <class 'float'>

Task: convert an int 0 to float

```
x = float(0)
print('x:', x, type(x))
```

x: 0.0 <class 'float'>

Task: convert an int 0 to str

```
x = str(0)
print('x:', x, type(x))
```

x: 0 <class 'str'>

Task: convert a float 0.1 to str

```
x = str(0.1)
print('x:', x, type(x))
```

x: 0.1 <class 'str'>

3.5 INTERACT WITH GENAI

Here are some questions and prompts you can interact with generative AI tools, including ChatGPT.

- What are variables in Python, and how are they used to store data? Provide examples with different data types like `str`, `int`, and `float`.
- What are the differences between `str`, `int`, and `float` data types in Python?
- Show how to declare variables in Python and assign values of different types.
- Create exercises to declare variables of different types (`str`, `int`, `float`) and use `print()` to display their values.
- Design an exercise to convert a string containing a number into an integer using `int()`, and perform arithmetic operations on it.
- Describe an error encountered when converting data types with `str()`, `int()`, or `float()` and ask, "Why did the error occur, and how can I avoid it in the future?"

## CHAPTER 4

Operations

W E have learned variables and data types, and now we can learn how to play with them! In Python, operations allow us to manipulate and combine values to perform various tasks. There are four main categories of operations: 1) Assignment operations, which establish the references we have experienced in the previous chapter; 2) Arithmetic operations, which enable us to perform mathematical calculations with numbers; 3) Relational operations, which enable us to make comparison and return `bool` values; and lastly 4) Logical operations, which enable us to play with `bool` values and get a compound condition. Let's get started!

4.1 ASSIGNMENT OPERATIONS

4.1.1 Explanation

In Python, the assignment operation is a fundamental concept that allows us to assign a value to a variable.

The assignment operation in Python is denoted by the equals sign (`=`). It is used to assign the value of an expression to a variable. When we assign a value to a variable, we are not copying the value itself, but rather the address of the value. This means that the variable now refers to the location in memory where the value is stored.

```python
x = 5 # x refers to the address of 5
print(x) # output 5
```

5

In this example, the value 5 is stored in memory, and the address of that value is assigned to the variable `x`. So, `x` now refers to the location in memory where the value 5 is stored.

When we assign the value of one variable to another variable, we are assigning the address that the first variable refers to, to the second variable.

DOI: 10.1201/9781003527725-4

```
y = x # y refers to the address that x refers to
print(y) # output 5
```

5

In this example, the address that x refers to (which is the location in memory where the value 5 is stored) is assigned to y. So, y now refers to the same location in memory as x, which is where the value 5 is stored. This means that both x and y now refer to the same value, which is 5.

If we change the value of x by assigning a different value to it, y will not change. This is because x and y are two separate variables that happen to point to the same location in memory initially. When we assign a new value to x, it will point to a new location in memory, but y will still point to the original location in memory.

```
x = 6 # x refers to the address of 6
print(y) # still output 5 since y still refers to 5
```

5

Multiple assignments in Python allow us to assign values to multiple variables in a single statement. This is a concise and readable way to assign values to multiple variables at once. For example:

```
x, y = 5, 6
```

This is equivalent to:

```
x = 5
y = 6
```

Here's how it works: The expressions on the right-hand side (5 and 6) are evaluated first. The values are then assigned to the variables on the left-hand side (x and y) in the order they are listed.

4.1.2 Practice

Task: Use two `input()` functions to get the name and age from the user, assign the name to **name**, convert age to int and assign it to **age**. Print a string as {name} is {age} years old.

```
name, age = input('What is your name: '), int(input('What is your age?'))
print(name, 'is', age, 'years old.')
```

```
What is your name: Neo
What is your age?18
Neo is 18 years old.
```

4.2 ARITHMETIC OPERATIONS

4.2.1 Explanation

Arithmetic operations in Python are used to perform mathematical calculations.

Here are the basic arithmetic operations supported by Python:

- Addition: a + b, adds two numbers a and b together.
- Subtraction: a - b, subtracts the number b from another number a.
- Multiplication: a * b, multiplies two numbers a and b together.
- Division: a / b, divides the number a by another number b and returns a `float` as the result.
- Floor Division: a // b, divides the number a by another number b and returns the largest whole number result as `int`.
- Modulus (remainder): a % b, returns the remainder of dividing the number a by another number b.
- Exponentiation: a ** b, raises the number a to the power of another number b.

4.2.2 Demonstration

```
a = 5
b = 2

print(a + b)    # Output: 7
print(a - b)    # Output: 3
print(a * b)    # Output: 10
print(a / b)    # Output: 2.5
print(a // b)   # Output: 2
print(a % b)    # Output: 1
print(a ** b)   # Output: 25
```

```
7
3
10
2.5
2
1
25
```

The precedence of arithmetic operations in Python determines the order in which operations are evaluated when there are multiple operations in an expression. Below is the precedence of arithmetic operations in Python, listed from highest to lowest:

- Parentheses (()): Evaluated first.
- Exponentiation (**): Evaluated next.
- Multiplication, Division, and Modulus (*, /, //, %): Evaluated next, from left to right.
- Addition and Subtraction (+, -): Evaluated next, from left to right.

```
result = 2 + 3 * (4 - 1)
print(result)   # Output: 11

result = (2 + 3) * 4
print(result)   # Output: 20

result = 2 ** 3 * 4
print(result)   # Output: 32
```

```
result = 10 / (2 ** 2)
print(result)  # Output: 2.5

result = 10 / 2 * 3
print(result)  # Output: 15

result = 10 * 2 + 3 % 4
print(result)  # Output: 23

result = 2 + 3 - 4
print(result)  # Output: 1

result = 10 - 2 + 3
print(result)  # Output: 11
```

```
11
20
32
2.5
15.0
23
1
11
```

4.2.3 Practice

Task: Evaluate following arithmatic operations, then code them to verify your evaluation:

```
2 + 3 * 4
(2 + 3) * 4
10 / 2 + 3
10 + 2 / 3
3 ** 2 * 4
(3 ** 2) * 4
12 / 3 - 2
12 - 3 / 2
2 + 3 * (4 - 1)
(2 + 3) * (4 - 1)
10 / (2 + 3)
10 - (2 + 3)
```

```
print(2 + 3 * 4) # 2 + 3 * 4 = 2 + 12 = 14
print((2 + 3) * 4) # (2 + 3) * 4 = 5 * 4 = 20
print(10 / 2 + 3) # 10 / 2 + 3 = 5.0 + 3 = 8.0
print(10 + 2 / 3) # 10 + 2 / 3 = 10 + 0.67 = 10.67
print(3 ** 2 * 4) # 3 ** 2 * 4 = 9 * 4 = 36
print((3 ** 2) * 4) # (3 ** 2) * 4 = 9 * 4 = 36
print(12 / 3 - 2) # 12 / 3 - 2 = 4.0 - 2 = 2.0
print(12 - 3 / 2) # 12 - 3 / 2 = 12 - 1.5 = 10.5
print(2 + 3 * (4 - 1)) # 2 + 3 * (4 - 1) = 2 + 3 * 3 = 2 + 9 = 11
print((2 + 3) * (4 - 1)) # (2 + 3) * (4 - 1) = 5 * 3 = 15
print(10 / (2 + 3)) # 10 / (2 + 3) = 10 / 5 = 2.0
print(10 - (2 + 3)) # 10 - (2 + 3) = 10 - 5 = 5
```

```
14
20
8.0
10.666666666666666
36
36
2.0
10.5
11
15
2.0
5
```

4.3   RELATIONAL OPERATIONS

4.3.1   Explanation

Relational operations in Python are used to compare values and determine if they meet certain conditions.

- Equal (==): a == b returns True if a is equal to b, and False otherwise. For example: 5 == 5 returns True, while 5 == 3 returns False.
- Not Equal (!=): a != b returns True if a is not equal to b, and False otherwise. For example: 5 != 3 returns True, while 5 != 5 returns False.
- Greater Than (>): a > b returns True if a is greater than b, and False otherwise. For example: 5 > 3 returns True, while 3 > 5 returns False.
- Less Than (<): a < b returns True if a is less than b, and False otherwise. For example: 3 < 5 returns True, while 5 < 3 returns False.
- Greater Than or Equal To (>=): a >= b returns True if a is greater than or equal to b, and False otherwise. For example: 5 >= 5 returns True, while 3 >= 5 returns False.
- Less Than or Equal To (<=): a <= b returns True if a is less than or equal to b, and False otherwise. Example: 3 <= 5 returns True, while 5 <= 3 returns False.

4.3.2   Practice

Task: Print out the comparison output of an operator. We can:

```
print(x, 'operator', y, 'is', x operator y)
```

where x and y are operands and **operator** is the operator. Then, assign x with 2, y with 3, then print out the comparison and result of

1. x > y
2. x >= y
3. x == y
4. x <= y
5. x < y
6. x != y

```
x = 2
y = 3
print(x, '>', y, 'is', x > y)
print(x, '>=', y, 'is', x >= y)
print(x, '==', y, 'is', x == y)
print(x, '<=', y, 'is', x <= y)
print(x, '<', y, 'is', x < y)
print(x, '!=', y, 'is', x != y)
```

```
2 > 3 is False
2 >= 3 is False
2 == 3 is False
2 <= 3 is True
2 < 3 is True
2 != 3 is True
```

Task: Ask the user to enter two integers, convert them to int, and assign them to x and y, print out the equation and result of

1. x > y
2. x >= y
3. x == y
4. x <= y
5. x < y
6. x != y

```
x = int(input('Enter an integer: '))
y = int(input('Enter another integer: '))
print(x, '>', y, 'is', x > y)
print(x, '>=', y, 'is', x >= y)
print(x, '==', y, 'is', x == y)
print(x, '<=', y, 'is', x <= y)
print(x, '<', y, 'is', x < y)
print(x, '!=', y, 'is', x != y)
```

```
Enter an integer: 2
Enter another integer: 3
2 > 3 is False
2 >= 3 is False
2 == 3 is False
2 <= 3 is True
2 < 3 is True
2 != 3 is True
```

4.4 LOGICAL OPERATIONS

4.4.1 Explanation

The results we get from relational operations, True and False, are the only two values of a data type, bool. Logical operations in Python are used to play with Boolean values, combine conditional statements, and evaluate the truthiness of expressions. There are three logical operations in Python:

- and (logical conjunction): a and b.
- or (logical disjunction): a or b.
- not (logical negation): not a.

We can learn and get familiar with the results of logical operations by examining the truth table shown in Table 4.1.

Table 4.1 Truth table for logical operations and, or, and not.

a	b	a and b	a or b	not a	not b
True	True	True	True	False	False
True	False	False	True	False	True
False	True	False	True	True	False
False	False	False	False	True	True

4.4.2 Practice

Task: Let's verify the truth table of logical operators. We can use the statement:

```
print(x, 'operator', y, 'is', x operator y)
```

where x and y are operands and **operator** is the operator. We can assign x with **True**, y with **False**, then print out the comparison and result of

1. x and x
2. x and y
3. y and x
4. y and y
5. x or x
6. x or y
7. y or x
8. y or y
9. not x
10. not y

```
x = True
y = False
print(x, 'and', x, 'is', x and x)
print(x, 'and', y, 'is', x and y)
print(y, 'and', x, 'is', y and x)
print(y, 'and', y, 'is', y and y)
print(x, 'or', x, 'is', x or x)
print(x, 'or', y, 'is', x or y)
print(y, 'or', x, 'is', y or x)
print(y, 'or', y, 'is', y or y)
print('not', x, 'is', not x)
print('not', y, 'is', not y)
```

```
True and True is True
True and False is False
False and True is False
```

```
False and False is False
True or True is True
True or False is True
False or True is True
False or False is False
not True is False
not False is True
```

The precedence of logical operations in Python is as follows:

- () (highest precedence).
- not.
- and.
- or (lowest precedence).

Task: Evaluate the following expressions and use code to verify your evaluation.

```
True and (True or False)
(True and False) or True
not (True and False)
not (False or True)
False and True or False and False or (False and True)
```

```
print(True and (True or False)) # True
print((True and False) or True) # True
print(not (True and False)) # True
print(not (False or True)) # False
print(False and True or False and False or (False and True)) # False
```

```
True
True
True
False
False
```

Task: A leap year, by definition, is a year that is a multiple of 4, except for years evenly divisible by 100 but not by 400. Ask user to give you a year, and print whether or not it is a leap year. Some test cases are:

```
input: 2000: True
input: 2100: False
input: 2024: True
input: 2023: False
```

```
year = int(input('Enter a year: '))
leap = year % 4 == 0 and year % 100 != 0 or year % 400 == 0
print(leap)
```

```
Enter a year: 2023
False
```

Let's summarize, compare, and contrast the operations in Table 4.2.

Table 4.2 Summary of Python operations.

Operation	Operator	Operand	Description
Arithmetic	`+, -, *, /, %, **, //`	`int, float`	Perform basic arithmetic operations: • `a + b` (addition) • `a - b` (subtraction) • `a * b` (multiplication) • `a / b` (division) • `a % b` (modulus) • `a ** b` (exponentiation) • `a // b` (floor division)
Relational	`==, !=, >, <, >=, <=`	Any comparable values	Compare values and return `True` or `False`: • `a == b` (equal to) • `a != b` (not equal to) • `a > b` (greater than) • `a < b` (less than) • `a >= b` (greater than or equal to) • `a <= b` (less than or equal to)
Logical	`and, or, not`	`bool`	Perform logical operations: • `a and b` (both conditions true) • `a or b` (either condition true) • `not a` (negates the condition)
Assignment	`=, +=, -=, *=, /=, %=, //=, **=`	Variables	Assign values or modify and assign: • `a = b` (assign) • `a += b` (add and assign) • `a -= b` (subtract and assign) • `a *= b` (multiply and assign) • `a /= b` (divide and assign) • `a %= b` (modulus and assign) • `a //= b` (floor divide and assign) • `a **= b` (exponentiate and assign)

4.5   INTERACT WITH GENAI

Here are some questions and prompts you can interact with generative AI tools, including ChatGPT.

- Demonstrate basic arithmetic operations like addition, subtraction, and division.
- Provide examples of relational operations such as >, <, and ==.
- Illustrate logical operations using and, or, and not.
- Combine different operations in a single statement to demonstrate operator precedence.
- What is the result of 5 // 2 and how is it different from 5 / 2?
- What happens if arithmetic, relational, and logical operators are used together in a statement?
- What are augmented assignment operators like +=, -=, and *=?
- What happens if you divide by zero in Python, and how can you handle it?
- Explain short-circuit evaluation in logical expressions with examples.
- How can you avoid confusion between = and ==?
- What issues might arise when combining relational and logical operations incorrectly?
- How can parentheses resolve precedence problems in complex expressions?
- What error occurs if you compare incompatible types like a string and a number?

## CHAPTER 5

String

How do you feel so far? You have learned a lot and practiced a lot. Don't stop! Let's learn something more interesting. Remember, we have used the data type `str` in our first Python program to display a string `'Hello, world!'` on the screen. Let's learn more about this very common data type and explore its built-in powerful functionalities in Python. We are going to learn how to create, access, slice, concatenate, and format strings, as well as the built-in functions of `str`.

Are you excited? Let's get started!

5.1 WHAT IS STR?

5.1.1 Explanation

In Python, a `str` (short for string) is a sequence of characters enclosed in quotations, such as `"Hello, world!"` or `'Hello, world!'`. Strings are a fundamental datatype in Python and are used to represent text, words, or phrases. They are important because they allow us to store and manipulate text data, which is essential for a wide range of applications, from simple text processing to complex natural language processing tasks. Strings are also used extensively in web development, data analysis, and machine learning, making them a crucial concept in Python.

5.1.2 Thinking

Think about in your real life, what scenarios you have to deal with strings, and what functionalities you wish you could do with it?

5.2 STRING CREATION

There are various approaches for creating or initializing a string object in Python.

DOI: 10.1201/9781003527725-5

5.2.1 Demonstration

You can create a string by enclosing a sequence of characters in quotations (either single, double, or triple quotations).

```
# Three strings below are equivalent
s1 = 'Hello, world!'
s2 = "Hello, world!"
s3 = '''Hello, world!'''
s1, s2, s3
```

```
('Hello, world!', 'Hello, world!', 'Hello, world!')
```

You can create a string from other data types, such as integers or floats, using the `str()` function.

```
# str() is a constructor, or initializor of strings
s4 = str(5)
s5 = str(6.0)
s6 = str(True)
s7 = str(False)
s4, s5, s6, s7
```

```
('5', '6.0', 'True', 'False')
```

You can use the `len()` function to obtain the length of a string, which is the number of characters in it.

```
print(s1, len(s1))
print(s7, len(s7))
```

```
Hello, world! 13
False 5
```

5.3   STRING ACCESS

You can access individual characters in a string using their index. In Python, the index always starts from 0. For a string variable `text`, the first character is then `text[0]` and the last character is then `text[len(text)-1]`. If you use an index larger than `len(text)-1`, you will get an error.

5.3.1   Demonstraton

For example (Figure 5.1):

```
text = 'Python'
first_char = text[0]   # Access the first character 'P'
print('First character:', first_char)
```

```
First character: P
```

```
last_char = text[len(text)-1]   # Access the last character 'n'
print('Last character:', last_char)
```

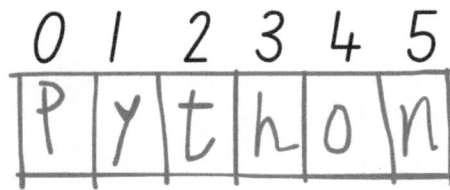

Figure 5.1 String non-negative index.

Last character: n

```
print(text[6]) # will result an error
```

```
---------------------------------------------------------------------
IndexError                              Traceback (most recent call last)
<ipython-input-6-c0ccc76c7160> in <cell line: 1>()
----> 1 print(text[6]) # will result an error

IndexError: string index out of range
```

The pythonic way of accessing the last element, rather than using `len(text)-1` as the index, is using `-1` directly as a negative index (Figure 5.2). You can think about that: while non-negative indices represent a string from the left to the right, negative indices represent the string from the right to the left. The rightmost character in the string `text` is `text[-1]` and the leftmost character is then `text[-len(text)]`. If you use an index smaller than `-len(text)`, you will get an error. For example:

```
last_char = text[-1]   # Access the last character 'n'
print('Last character:', last_char)
```

Last character: n

```
first_char = text[-len(text)]   # Access the first character 'P'
print('First character:', first_char)
```

First character: P

```
print(text[-7]) # will result an error
```

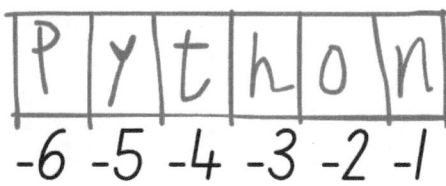

Figure 5.2 String negative index.

```
--------------------------------------------------------------------------
IndexError                                    Traceback (most recent call last)
<ipython-input-11-8273384d22fe> in <cell line: 1>()
----> 1 print(text[-7]) # will result an error

IndexError: string index out of range
```

5.3.2 Practice

Given a string `'Learning is fun!'`, and practice the small tasks below.

```
# Run this cell for the practices
text = 'Learning is fun!'
```

Task: Print the length of `text`

```
print(len(text))
```

16

Task: Print the first character of `text` using a non-negative index

```
print(text[0])
```

L

Task: Print the last character of `text` using a non-negative index

```
print(text[len(text)-1])
```

!

Task: Print the second character of `text` using a non-negative index

```
print(text[1])
```

e

Task: Print the second to last character of `text` using a non-negative index

```
print(text[len(text)-2])
```

n

Task: Print the last character of `text` using a negative index

```
print(text[-1])
```

!

Task: Print the first character of `text` using a negative index

```
print(text[-len(text)])
```

L

Task: Print the second to last character of `text` using a negative index

```
print(text[-2])
```

n

Task: Print the second character of `text` using a negative index

```
print(text[-len(text)+1])
```

e

Task: Try to get a `string index out of range` error using positive index

```
print(text[len(text)])
```

```
---------------------------------------------------------------------
IndexError                                Traceback (most recent call last)
<ipython-input-11-94a4b90f352f> in <cell line: 1>()
----> 1 print(text[len(text)])
```

\enlargethispage*{40pt}

```
IndexError: string index out of range
```

Task: Try to get a `string index out of range` error using negative index

```
print(text[-len(text)-1])
```

```
---------------------------------------------------------------------
IndexError                                Traceback (most recent call last)
<ipython-input-12-a21546afe548> in <cell line: 1>()
----> 1 print(text[-len(text)-1])
```

```
IndexError: string index out of range
```

5.4 STRING SLICING

If you want to obtain a portion of a string, you can use string slicing. It's done using the [start:stop:step] notation in place of the indices, where the start represents the index to start slicing, the stop represents the index to stop slicing (thus, the character of this index will be excluded from the substring), and the step represents the step value (which is 1 by default) in the slicing (Figure 5.3, 5.4).

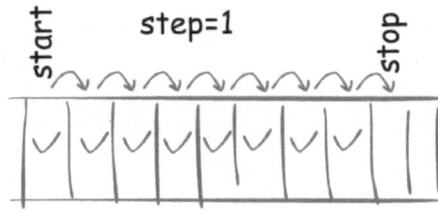

Figure 5.3 String slicing with step as 1.

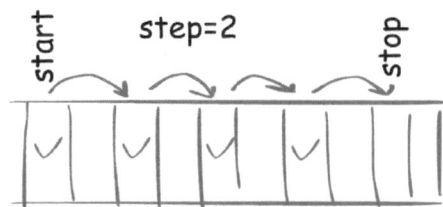

Figure 5.4 String slicing with step as 2.

5.4.1 Demonstration

```
text = 'Python is amazing'
print(len(text))
```

17

```
sub = text[0:6]  # Extracts 'Python'
print('Substring:', sub)
```

Substring: Python

```
sub = text[10:17]  # Extracts 'amazing'
print('Substring:', sub)
```

Substring: amazing

```
sub = text[:6]  # Extracts 'Python'
print('Substring:', sub)
```

Substring: Python

```
sub = text[10:]  # Extracts 'amazing'
print('Substring:', sub)
```

Substring: amazing

```
sub = text[:]  # Extracts everthing
print('Substring:', sub)
```

Substring: Python is amazing

```
sub = text[-7:]  # Extracts 'amazing'
print('Substring:', sub)
```

Substring: amazing

```
sub = text[:6:2]  # Extracts 'Pto'
print('Substring:', sub)
```

Substring: Pto

```
sub = text[10::2]  # Extracts 'aaig'
print('Substring:', sub)
```

Substring: aaig

```
sub = text[::5]  # Extracts 'Pnan'
print('Substring:', sub)
```

Substring: Pnan

```
sub = text[::-1]  # Extracts 'gnizama si nohtyP'
print('Substring:', sub)
```

Substring: gnizama si nohtyP

5.4.2   Practice

Given a string 'Learning is fun', and practice the small tasks below.

```
# Run this cell for the practices
text = 'Learning is fun'
```

Task: Slice Learning from the text

```
print(text[:8])
```

Learnin

Task: Slice fun from the text

```
print(text[-3:])
```

fun

Task: Slice is from the text

```
print(text[9:-4])
```

is

Task: Slice the characters with index 0, 5, 10, ... from the text

```
print(text[::5])
```

Lis

Task: Starting from index 2, end at index 10, slice every other character from the text

```
print(text[2:10:2])
```

ann

5.5   STRING CONCATENATION

5.5.1   Demonstration

There are various ways of concatenating strings together.

```
# Using the + Operator
text = 'Hello' + ', world!'
print(text)
```

Hello, world!

```
# Using the += Operator
text = 'Hello'
text += ', world!' # the same as text = text + ', world!'
print(text)
```

Hello, world!

String concatenations require two `str` objects as operands. Not like C++ and Java, Python will not auto-convert other data types to `str` for concatenation. For example:

```
# Python wont auto-convert other data types to str

text = 18 + ' years old' # will result an error
print(text)
```

```
-------------------------------------------------------------------------
TypeError                                 Traceback (most recent call last)
<ipython-input-57-58e6c2aaf484> in <cell line: 3>()
      1 # Python wont auto-convert other data types to str
      2
----> 3 text = 18 + ' years old' # will result an error
      4 print(text)

TypeError: unsupported operand type(s) for +: 'int' and 'str'
```

```
# Python wont auto-convert other data types to str

text = str(18) + ' years old' # Convert int to str before concatenation
print(text)
```

18 years old

5.6 STRING FORMAT

If you have many substrings, concatenating them together is not easy to do and not friendly to read. Actually, Python offers multiple ways to combine multiple substrings together through string formatting. String formatting is a powerful feature in Python that allows you to insert values into a string template. There are two main ways to do this: using the `.format()` method and using `f-strings`.

5.6.1 Demonstration

You can format a string by using `.format()`:

```
# Assign the string 'Alice' to the variable name
name = 'Alice'

# Assign the value 30 to the variable age
```

```
age = 30

# Create a formatted string using name and age
formatted_str = 'Name: {}, Age: {}'.format(name, age)

# Print the formatted string
print(formatted_str)
```

```
Name: Alice, Age: 30
```

You can also format a string by using **f-strings** (**f''**):

```
name = 'Bob'
age = 25
formatted_str = f'Name: {name}, Age: {age}'
print(formatted_str)
```

```
Name: Bob, Age: 25
```

It is very convenient when you combine **input()** for part of the output:

```
name = input('What is your name? ')
print(f'Hello, {name}!')
```

```
What is your name? Neo
Hello, Neo!
```

You can also control the details of the format of the output string:

```
a = 3.1415926
print(f'Zero decimal points of a float: {a:.0f}')
print(f'Two decimal points of a float: {a:.2f}')
print(f'Four decimal points of a float: {a:.4f}')
```

```
Zero decimal points of a float: 3
Two decimal points of a float: 3.14
Four decimal points of a float: 3.1416
```

```
b = 3
print(f'Make up length of 2 by adding extra zeroes: {b:02d}')
print(f'Make up length of 4 by adding extra zeroes: {b:04d}')
print(f'Make up length of 8 by adding extra zeroes: {b:08d}')
```

```
Make up length of 2 by adding extra zeroes: 03
Make up length of 4 by adding extra zeroes: 0003
Make up length of 8 by adding extra zeroes: 00000003
```

```
c = 31415926
print(f'Print scientific notation of a number: {a:e}')
print(f'Print scientific notation of a number: {b:e}')
print(f'Print scientific notation of a number: {c:e}')
```

```
Print scientific notation of a number: 3.141593e+00
Print scientific notation of a number: 3.000000e+00
Print scientific notation of a number: 3.141593e+07
```

5.6.2   Practice

Task: Use f-strings to print the following string:

```
My name is John,
I am 30 years old, and
I live in New York.
```

where `John`, `30`, and `New York` are values you get from users.

```
print(f'''
My name is {input('What is your name? ')},
I am {input('What is your age? ')}, and
I live in {input('Where do you live? ')}.
''')
```

```
What is your name? John
What is your age? 30
Where do you live? New York

My name is John,
I am 30, and
I live in New York.
```

Task: Get the price of a book from the user, and use f-strings to print the following string: `'The price of the book is ${price}'`.

```
price = input('Enter the price of the book: ')
print(f'The price of the book is ${price}')
```

```
Enter the price of the book: 32.30
The price of the book is $32.30
```

Task: Let `a` and `b` be two integers you get from the user, use f-strings to print the result of arithmetic operations +, -, *, /, //, %, and **. For example, if the user enters `a = 1`, `b = 3`, you'll print:

```
When a = 1, b = 3:
1 + 3 = 4
1 - 3 = -2
1 * 3 = 3
1 / 3 = 0.3333333333333333
1 // 3 = 0
1 % 3 = 1
1 ** 3 = 1
```

```
a = 1
b = 3
print(f'''When a = {a}, b = {b}:
{a} + {b} = {a+b}
{a} - {b} = {a-b}
{a} * {b} = {a*b}
{a} / {b} = {a/b}
{a} // {b} = {a//b}
{a} % {b} = {a%b}
```

```
{a} ** {b} = {a**b}
''')
```

```
When a = 1, b = 3:
1 + 3 = 4
1 - 3 = -2
1 * 3 = 3
1 / 3 = 0.3333333333333333
1 // 3 = 0
1 % 3 = 1
1 ** 3 = 1
```

5.7   USEFUL FUNCTIONS

As one of the most important data types, `str` has many built-in functions to support its wide usage. We are going to briefly introduce some of them here.

5.7.1   Demonstration

```
text = 'Python is versatile.'
```

Case conversion:

```
# Uppercase, lowercase, and titlecase
upper_text = text.upper()
lower_text = text.lower()
title_text = text.title()
print('text:', text)
print('upper_text:', upper_text)
print('lower_text:', lower_text)
print('title_text:', title_text)
```

```
text: Python is versatile.
upper_text: PYTHON IS VERSATILE.
lower_text: python is versatile.
title_text: Python Is Versatile.
```

Checking if a string starts or ends with a specific substring:

```
# Checking if a string starts or ends with a specific substring
starts_with = text.startswith('Python')
print(f'{text} starts_with Python? is {starts_with}')
ends_with = text.endswith('.')
print(f'{text} end with .? is {ends_with}')
```

```
Python is versatile. starts_with Python? is True
Python is versatile. end with .? is True
```

```
token = 'python'
print(f'{text} starts_with {token}? is {text.startswith(token)}')
```

```
Python is versatile. starts_with python? is False
```

```
token = 'versatile'
print(f'{text} ends_with {token}? is {text.endswith(token)}')
```

Python is versatile. ends_with versatile? is False

Replacing a substring:

```
# Replacing a substring
replaced_text = text.replace('versatile', 'powerful')
print('replaced_text:', replaced_text)
```

replaced_text: Python is powerful.

Splitting a string into a list:

```
# Splitting a string into a list
split_text = text.split() # the default delimeter is a space
print('split_text:', split_text)
```

split_text: ['Python', 'is', 'versatile.']

```
split_text = text.split('s')
print('split_text:', split_text)
```

split_text: ['Python i', ' ver', 'atile.']

Finding the position of a substring:

```
# Finding the position of a substring
position = text.find('i')
print(position)
```

7

```
position = text.find('i', 8)
print(position)
```

16

```
position = text.find('i', 17)
print(position)
```

-1

```
position = text.rfind('i')
print(position)
```

16

Stripping whitespace from the beginning and end:

```
# Stripping whitespace from the beginning
stripped_text = '    whitespace    '.lstrip()
print(f'Left stripped_text: ---{stripped_text}---')

# Stripping whitespace from the end
stripped_text = '    whitespace    '.rstrip()
print(f'Right stripped_text: ---{stripped_text}---')
```

```
Left stripped_text: ---whitespace    ---
Right stripped_text: ---    whitespace---
```

```
# Stripping whitespace from the beginning and end
stripped_text = '    whitespace    '.strip()
print(f'Stripped_text: ---{stripped_text}---')
```

```
Stripped_text: ---whitespace---
```

5.7.2 Practice

```
# run this cell for following tasks
text = 'Everyday is a great day'
```

Task: Convert the string **text** to uppercase and print it out.

```
print(text.upper())
```

```
EVERYDAY IS A GREAT DAY
```

Task: Convert the string **text** to lowercase and print it out.

```
print(text.lower())
```

```
everyday is a great day
```

Task: Convert the string **text** to titlecase and print it out.

```
print(text.title())
```

```
Everyday Is A Great Day
```

Task: Check if the string **text** starts with **'Everyday'**

```
print(text.startswith('Everyday'))
```

```
True
```

Task: Check if the string **text** starts with **'Each'**

```
print(text.startswith('Each'))
```

```
False
```

Task: Check if the string **text** ends with **'day'**

```
print(text.endswith('day'))
```

```
True
```

Task: Check if the string **text** ends with **'day!'**

```
print(text.endswith('day!'))
```

```
False
```

Task: replace `'great'` in the string `text` with `'wonderful'`

```
print(text.replace('great', 'wonderful'))
```

Everyday is a wonderful day

Task: split the string `text`

```
print(text.split())
```

['Everyday', 'is', 'a', 'great', 'day']

Task: split the string `text` by `'e'`

```
print(text.split('e'))
```

['Ev', 'ryday is a gr', 'at day']

Task: Find the first occurance of 'day' in the string `text`

```
print(text.find('day'))
```

5

Task: Find the second occurance of 'day' in the string `text`

```
print(text.find('day', 6))
```

20

Task: Find the last occurance of 'day' in the string `text`

```
print(text.rfind('day'))
```

20

Task: Removing the leading spaces of '   Everday is a wonderful day   '

```
print('     Everday is a wonderful day      '.lstrip())
```

Everday is a wonderful day

Task: Removing the ending spaces of '   Everday is a wonderful day   '

```
print('     Everday is a wonderful day      '.rstrip())
```

    Everday is a wonderful day

Task: Removing the surrounding spaces of '   Everday is a wonderful day   ' from both ends

```
print('     Everday is a wonderful day      '.strip())
```

Everday is a wonderful day

Let's summarize commonly used string operations in Table 5.1.

Table 5.1 Summary of Python string methods.

Method	Description	Example
`str.upper()`	Converts all characters to uppercase.	`"hello".upper()` → `"HELLO"`
`str.lower()`	Converts all characters to lowercase.	`"HELLO".lower()` → `"hello"`
`str.capitalize()`	Capitalizes the first character of the string.	`"hello world".capitalize()` → `"Hello world"`
`str.title()`	Capitalizes the first letter of each word.	`"hello world".title()` → `"Hello World"`
`str.strip()`	Removes leading and trailing whitespaces.	`" hello ".strip()` → `"hello"`
`str.replace (old, new)`	Replaces occurrences of a substring with another substring.	`"hello world".replace ("world", "Python")` → `"hello Python"`
`str.split(sep)`	Splits the string into a list based on a delimiter.	`"a,b,c".split(",")` → `["a", "b", "c"]`
`str.join(iterable)`	Joins elements of an iterable with the string as the delimiter.	`",".join(["a", "b", "c"])` → `"a,b,c"`
`str.find(sub)`	Returns the lowest index of the substring or −1 if not found.	`"hello".find("e")` → 1
`str.startswith (prefix)`	Checks if the string starts with the specified prefix.	`"hello".startswith ("he")` → True
`str.endswith (suffix)`	Checks if the string ends with the specified suffix.	`"hello".endswith("lo")` → True
`str.isdigit()`	Checks if all characters are digits.	`"123".isdigit()` → True
`str.isalpha()`	Checks if all characters are alphabetic.	`"abc".isalpha()` → True
`str.count(sub)`	Counts occurrences of a substring in the string.	`"banana".count("a")` → 3

5.8 INTERACT WITH GENAI

Here are some questions and prompts you can interact with generative AI tools, including ChatGPT.

- Explain how strings can be accessed using indices. What is the difference between non-negative and negative indices?
- Explain the purpose of f-strings and their advantages for string formatting.
- Use an f-string to format a message with variables.
- How do negative indices work for slicing? For example, what does `s[-3:-1]` return?
- What happens when you concatenate a string with a number without converting the number?
- How does the `replace()` method work? Provide an example.
- How can you count the number of occurrences of a character in a string?
- How can you use slicing to reverse a string?
- Create a program that accepts a user's full name and displays it in reverse order (last name first).
- Write a script to count the number of vowels in a given string.
- Use slicing to check if a string is a palindrome.
- What causes an `IndexError` when accessing string elements, and how can you avoid it?
- Why does slicing not throw an error even if the indices are out of range?
- Why does modifying a character in a string cause an error, and what is the workaround?

## CHAPTER 6

Case Studies of Python Fundamentals

W$_{\text{E}}$ have learned a lot of concepts in this section! From the general understanding of Python, to the first Python program, from the built-in data types and to dynamically typed variables, from the various operations to the detailed exploration of `str`, you mastered the fundamentals of Python successfully! Let's apply what we just learned to some real-life cases and see how Python can assist us in solving problems. These case studies are designed to test your understanding of input and output, variables, operations, and `str` in Python.

For these real-life cases, you should use `input()` to get the user to enter the information and use `print()` to print the information on the screen. At this moment, we can assume users will follow instructions carefully – they will enter the valid inputs as required.

Are you ready? Let's get started!

6.1 SIMPLE CHECK OUT

Instruction: You are going to program a super simple check-out system for a store. This store has an interesting rule that every customer can only buy one product (the quantity of the product is not limited) in one order.

1. Ask the user to enter the price/unit of the product (it should be a float)
2. Ask the user to enter the quantity of the product (it should be an integer)
3. We have a sales tax of 6.25%
4. Calculate and display the total amount of this order (for example, 59.25)
5. Ask the user to enter the amount of bills paid (for example, 60)
6. Calculate and display the change (for example, 0.75)

DOI: 10.1201/9781003527725-6

```
# Prompt the user to enter the price and convert it to a float
price = float(input('What is the price per unit of the product? '))

# Prompt the user to enter the quantity and convert it to an integer
quantity = int(input('What is the quantity of the product? '))

# Calculate the total amount including a 6.25% tax
total = price * quantity * (1 + 0.0625)

# Print the total amount, formatted to 2 decimal places
print(f'The total amount of this order with tax is ${total:.2f}')

# Prompt the user to enter the amount paid and convert it to a float
paid = float(input('What is the amount of bill paid?  '))

# Calculate the change to be returned
change = paid - total

# Print the change amount, formatted to 2 decimal places
print(f'The change is ${change:.2f}')
```

```
What is the price per unit of the product? 25.99
What is the quantity of the product? 12
The total amount of this order with tax is $331.37
What is the amount of bill paid?  350
The change is $18.63
```

6.2   TIPS SPLIT

Instruction: You are going to program a super simple tip split system.

1. Ask the user to enter the total amount of meal before tax (it should be a float)
2. Ask the user to enter the number of people to split the tips (it should be an integer)
3. We have a sales tax of 6.25%, and we tip at 18%
4. Calculate and display the total amount due (including tax and tips)
5. Calculate and display the amount each person should pay.

```
# Prompt the user to enter the total before tax and convert it to a float
total = float(input('What is the total amount of the meal before tax? '))

# Prompt the user to enter the number of people and convert it to an int
num = int(input('How many people to split the tips? '))

tax = 0.0625   # Set the tax rate as 6.25%
tip = 0.18   # Set the tip percentage as 18%

# Calculate the total amount due, including tax and tip
total_due = total * (1 + tax + tip)

# Calculate the amount each person owes
each_due = total_due / num
```

```
# Print the total amount due and the amount each person owes
print(f'Total due is ${total_due:.2f}. Each due is ${each_due:.2f}')
```

```
What is the total amount of the meal before tax? 124
How many people to split the tips? 5
Total due is $154.07. Each due is $30.81
```

6.3 COMPOUND INTEREST

Instruction: You are going to program a super simple compound interest calculator.

1. Ask the user to enter the amount saved right now (it should be a float)
2. Ask the user to enter the number of years(it should be an integer)
3. Ask the user to enter the interest rate (it should be a float number, and 0.03 represents 3%)
4. Calculate and display the total amount after these years

```
# Prompt the user to enter the current savings and convert it to a float
saving = float(input('What is the amount of saving right now? '))

# Prompt the user to enter the years and convert it to an integer
years = int(input('What is the number of years? '))

# Prompt the user to enter the interest rate and convert it to a float
rate = float(input('What is the interest rate per year?  '))

# Calculate the total amount over the given years
total = saving * (1 + rate) ** years

# Print the total amount after the given years
print(f'The total amount after these years is: ${total:.2f}')
```

```
What is the amount of saving right now? 100000
What is the number of years? 10
What is the interest rate per year?  0.05
The total amount after these years is: $162889.46
```

II

Flow Control and Functions

SECTION II: FLOW CONTROL AND FUNCTIONS covers how Python handles flow control, enabling you to create dynamic and responsive programs. You'll explore the fundamentals of branching and repetition, the core mechanisms that allow your code to make decisions and execute tasks repeatedly. Building on these basics, we introduce functions, an advanced yet essential tool for managing code flow more efficiently. You'll learn how to define functions with no parameters, one parameter, and multiple parameters, as well as how to use return values to retrieve results from functions. The section also covers how functions can call other functions, including the concept of recursion, where a function calls itself to solve problems that require repetitive processing.

By the end of this section, you will be able to:

- Understand and apply branching and repetition for basic flow control in Python.

- Define and use functions to organize and simplify your code.

- Create functions with varying numbers of parameters to handle different input scenarios.

- Utilize return values to obtain and use results from functions.

- Understand default values in functions and use keywords to pass arguments.

- Implement recursive functions and understand how they solve complex problems through repetition.

## CHAPTER 7

Branching

F LOW CONTROL is a fundamental concept in programming that allows you to control the order in which your code is executed. In Python, the flow control statements are used to deviate from the sequential flow of a program. In sequential flow, the code is executed line by line, from top to bottom, in the order it is written. Each statement is executed in sequence, and the program follows a straightforward, linear path. On the other hand, flow control statements allow you to alter the sequential flow of a program. They enable you to branch to different parts of the program based on conditions (branching), repeat certain statements or blocks of code (looping), and even skip certain statements or blocks of code (skipping).

In Python, the main flow control statements are:

- `if-elif-else` statements (branching).
- `for` loops (repetition).
- `while` loops (repetition).
- `break` and `continue` statements (skipping).
- `try-except` statements (error handling).

We will learn branching in this chapter. Are you excited? Let's get started!

7.1 OPTIONAL BRANCHING

Optional branching (`if`) allows you to execute a block of code only if a certain condition is true (Figure 7.1).

DOI: 10.1201/9781003527725-7

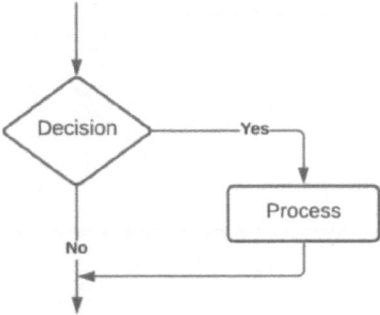

Figure 7.1   A flow chart for optional branching.

7.1.1   Demonstration

The general syntax of an optional branching is:

```
if condition:
  statements
```

Here, the keyword `if` initiates the branching clause. The `condition` determines the evaluation, resulting in a Boolean value, either `True` or `False`. The `:` completes the clause. In the next line, an indentation of two spaces `' '` indicates that the `statements` within this line are enclosed by the `if` clause. Execution of the statements occurs only when the `condition` evaluates to `True`.

```
x = 5
```

```
if x < 0:
  print('x is negative!')
```

In this instance, the statement is to print a string `'x is negative!'`. However, since we know `x` is 5 and `5 < 0` evaluates to `False`, nothing will be printed.

Let's observe more examples.

```
if x >10:
  print('x is more than 10!')
```

```
if x % 2 == 0:
  print('x is even!')
```

```
if x > 0:
  print('x is positive!')
```

```
x is positive!
```

```
if x %2 != 0:
  print('x is odd!')
```

```
x is odd!
```

```
degree = 72
if degree < 60 or degree > 80:
  print('Not good for hiking!')
```

```
if degree >= 60 and degree <= 80:
  print('Enjoy the hiking!')
```

Enjoy the hiking!

7.1.2 Practice

Task: Check if a number is even. You should ask the user to enter an integer, if it is an even number, print `'it is even'`; otherwise, print nothing. Hint: to test if a number is even, we need to use %2 and check if the reminder is 0 or not. If it is 0, then the number is even.

```
n = int(input('Please enter an integer: '))
if n % 2 == 0:
  print('It is even')
```

Please enter an integer: 3

Task: Check if a number is odd. Similar to the task above. However, this time, you only print `'It is odd'` when the number entered is odd.

```
n = int(input('Please enter an integer: '))
if n % 2 != 0:
  print('It is odd')
```

Please enter an integer: 3
It is odd

Task: Check if a number is divisible by 6. You should ask the user to enter an integer, if it is dividable by 6, print `'It can be divisible by 6'`.

```
n = int(input('Please enter an integer: '))
if n % 6 == 0:
  print('It can be dividable by 6')
```

Please enter an integer: 23

Task: Check if an input is `'STOP'`. Ask the user to enter some words, and only when the user entered `'STOP'`, you print `'Bye'`.

```
word = input('Enter some word: ')
if word == 'STOP':
  print('Bye')
```

Enter some word: STOP
Bye

Task: Ask the user to enter some words, and only when the user entered any case combination of `'stop'`, for example, `'stop'`, `'Stop'`, `'STOP'`, etc., you print `'Bye'`.

```
word = input('Enter some word: ').upper()
if word == 'STOP':
  print('Bye')
```

```
Enter some word: stop
Bye
```

Task: Password Setup. Ask the user to enter a password twice, if the second input matches the first one, print `'You are all set'`

```
password1 = input('Enter a new password:')
password2 = input('Enter the password again:')
if password1 == password2:
  print('You are all set')
```

```
Enter a new password:12
Enter the password again:12
You are all set
```

7.2 ALTERNATIVE BRANCHING

Alternative branching allows you to execute one block of code if a condition is true, and another block of code if the condition is false (Figure 7.2).

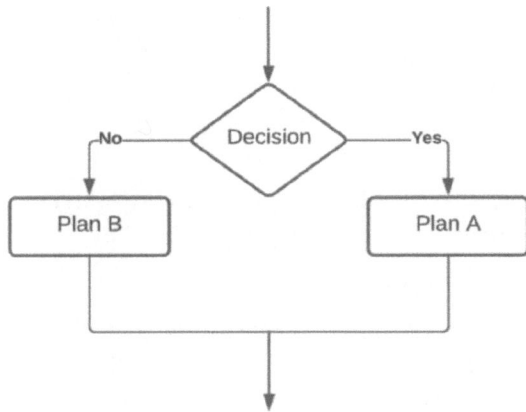

Figure 7.2 A flow chart for alternative branching.

7.2.1 Demonstration

The general syntax of an alternative branching is:

```
if condition:
  statements
else:
  statements
```

Here, the keyword `if` initiates the branching clause, which is exactly the same as the optional branching. The alternative branching has the extra, which is the keyword else and the associated clause. The else clause doesn't need a condition, since the condition is by default when the condition in the if clause evaluates to False. The statements enclosed by the else clause share the same indentation. Execution of the statements occurs only when the condition evaluates to False.

```
x = 5
```

```
if x <= 0:
  print('x is non-positive!')
else:
  print('x is positive!')
```

x is positive!

```
if x %2 == 0:
  print('x is even!')
else:
  print('x is odd!')
```

x is odd!

```
if x == 2 or x == 3 or x == 5 or x == 7:
  print('x is a prime number.')
else:
  print('x is not a prime number.')
```

x is a prime number.

7.2.2 Practice

Task: Check if the weather is good for hiking. You should ask the user to enter a float value as the temperature in Fahrenheit.

- If the temperature is within [60, 80], print 'Perfect';
- otherwise, print 'Not that good'.

```
temp = float(input('Please enter the temperature in Fahrenheit: '))
if temp < 60 or temp > 80:
  print('Not that good')
else:
  print('Perfect')
```

```
temp = float(input('Please enter the temperature in Fahrenheit: '))
if temp >= 60 and temp <= 80:
  print('Perfect')
else:
  print('Not that good')
```

Task: Check if the user feels happy. You should ask the user 'Are you happy now?'.

- If the user enters 'Yes', print "Fantastic!"
- otherwise, print 'How can I help?'

```
happy = input('Are you happy now? Yes or No:')
if happy == 'Yes':
  print('Fantastic!')
else:
  print('How can I help?')
```

```
Are you happy now? Yes or No:Yes
Fantastic!
```

Task: Check if your plants need water. You should ask the user to enter an integer indicating the level of moisture of the soil (from 1: super dry; to 10: super wet).

- If the level is below 3, print 'Yes, you should water your plants now'
- otherwise, print 'No. Wait for the soil to be dryer'.

```
level = int(input('''Enter the level of moisture of the soil
(from 1: super dry; to 10: super wet):'''))
if level < 3:
  print('Yes, you should water your plants now')
else:
  print('No. Wait for the soil to be dryer')
```

Task: Check if a student finished this lab

At first, ask the user:'Do you care about your learning outcome?'

- If yes, ask the user 'Have your finished this lab?' If yes, print 'Good job!'. If no, print 'Get it done ASAP!!!!!!'
- If no, then print 'As long as you are happy.'

```
care = input('Do you care about your learning outcome? Yes or No:')
if care == 'Yes':
  finish = input('Have your finished this lab? ')
  if finish == 'Yes':
    print('Good job!')
  else:
    print('Get it done ASAP!!!!!!')
else:
  print('As long as you are happy.')
```

```
Do you care about your learning outcome? Yes or No:Yes
Have your finished this lab? No
Get it done ASAP!!!!!!
```

7.3 MULTIPLE BRANCHING

Multiple branching allows you to check multiple conditions and execute different blocks of code based on which condition is true (Figure 7.3).

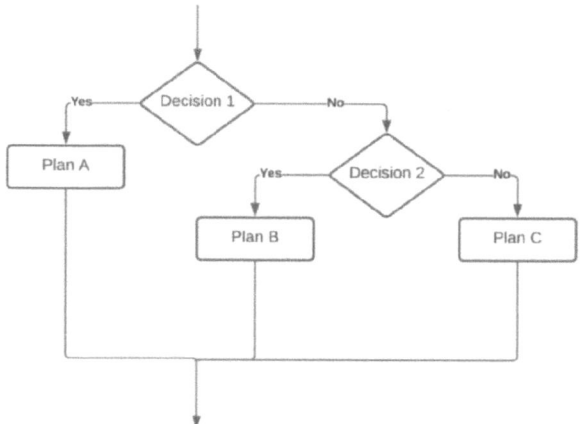

Figure 7.3 A flow chart for multiple branching.

7.3.1 Demonstration

The general syntax of multiple branching is:

```
if condition1:
    statements
elif condition2:
    statements
else:
    statements
```

Here, the keyword `if` initiates a branching clause, which is the same as an optional branching clause. The keyword `elif` initiates another clause when `condition1` evaluates to `False`, with another `condition2`. If `condition2` evaluates to `True`, the statements enclosed by the `elif` will be executed. Otherwise, the flow moves to the next `elif` clause or to the `else` clause. It's worth noting that the `else` clause is optional, meaning you don't always have to include an `else` clause in multiple branching.

```
x = 10
if x > 10:
    print('x is greater than 10')
elif x == 10:
    print('x is equal to 10')
else:
    print('x is less than 10')
```

```
x is equal to 10
```

```
if x%2 == 0:
    print('x is divisible by 2')
elif x%3 == 0:
    print('x is divisible by 3')
```

```
x is divisible by 2
```

```
if x%2 == 0:
  if x%3 == 0:
    print('x is divisible by 6')
  elif x%5 == 0:
    print('x is divisible by 10')
else:
  print('x is odd')
```

```
x is divisible by 10
```

```
x = int(input('Please enter a point-based grade in 0-100:'))
if x >= 90:
  print('A')
elif x >= 80:
  print('B')
elif x >= 70:
  print('C')
elif x >= 60:
  print('D')
elif x >= 0:
  print('F')
```

```
Please enter a point-based grade in 0-100:-1
```

7.3.2   Practice

Task: Check if a number is positive, negative, or 0. You should ask the user to enter a number, if it is above 0, print 'It is positive'; if it is below 0, print 'It is negative'; otherwise, print 'It is zero'.

```
n = float(input('Enter a number: '))
if n > 0:
  print('It is positive')
elif n < 0:
  print('It is negative')
else:
  print('It is zero')
```

```
Enter a number: 2
It is positive
```

Task: Check how many days the current month has. You should ask the user to enter the number indicating the current month, such as 1 for January; then print the days the month has, such as print 31 if the user entered 1. Let's assume there are 28 days in February.

```
month = int(input('Enter the month: 1 - 12:'))
if (month == 1 or month == 3 or month == 5 or month == 7
    or month == 8 or month == 10 or month == 12):
  print(31)
elif month == 2:
  print(28)
else:
  print(30)
```

```
Enter the month: 1 - 12:2
28
```

Task: A parking garage has following price policy:

1. first half hour: 5
2. second half hour to 2 hours: 15
3. more than 2 hours: 5 per hour

Ask the user to enter the hours of parking (it should be a float number, such as 1.6 as 1.6 hours), and calculate the parking fee. Note, if a user parks the car for 5.5 hours, the formular will be 5 (for first half hour) + 15 (for a second half hour to 2 hours) + 5 * (5.5 - 2) (for hours more than 2)

```python
hours = float(input('Enter the hours of parking as a float number:'))
if hours <= 0.5:
    fee = 5
elif hours <= 2:
    fee = 5 + 15
else:
    fee = 5 + 15 + 5 * (hours - 2)
print(fee)
```

```
Enter the hours of parking as a float: 5.5
37.5
```

Task: Write a program that asks the user to enter a person's age. The program should display a message indicating whether the person is an infant, a child, a teenager, an adult, or a senior citizen. The following are the guidelines:

1. If the person is 1 year old or less, he or she is an infant.
2. If the person is older than 1 year, but younger than 13 years, he or she is a child.
3. If the person is at least 13 years old, but less than 20 years old, he or she is a teenager.
4. If the person is at least 20 years old, but less than 65 years old, he or she is an adult.
5. Otherwise, the person is a senior citizen.

```python
age = int(input('Enter your age as an integer: '))
if age <= 1:
    print('You are an infant')
elif age < 13:
    print('You are a child')
elif age < 20:
    print('You are a teenager')
elif age < 65:
    print('You are an adult')
else:
    print('You are a senior citizen')
```

7.4   CASE STUDIES OF BRANCHING

These case studies are designed to test your understanding of flow control: branching. We are going to create some simple programs using these tools. You will find some real-life tasks in the sections below. At this moment, we can assume users will follow instructions carefully – they will enter the valid inputs as required.

7.4.1   What day is today?

Write a program that asks the user for a number in the range of 1 through 7. The program should display the corresponding day of the week, where:

- 1 = Monday,
- 2 = Tuesday,
- 3 = Wednesday,
- 4 = Thursday,
- 5 = Friday,
- 6 = Saturday,
- 7 = Sunday, and
- all other values entered = ERROR

```python
day = input('What day is today? 1 - 7:')
if day == '1':
  print('Monday')
elif day == '2':
  print('Tuesday')
elif day == '3':
  print('Wednesday')
elif day == '4':
  print('Thursday')
elif day == '5':
  print('Friday')
elif day == '6':
  print('Saturday')
elif day == '7':
  print('Sunday')
else:
  print('ERROR')
```

```
What day is today? 1 - 7:4
Thursday
```

7.4.2   Tax calculator

You are going to program a simple tax calculator.

Step1: Ask the user to enter the gross income of year.

Step2: Calculate the tax based on the following formula:

1. No more than $100,000, one pays just 1%
2. No more than $100,000 one pays 5%

3. More than $500,000 then one pays 5% tax on the first 500,000 and 2 cents for every dollar above 500,000

Step3: Print the tax amount on the screen.

```python
# Prompt the user to enter the gross income
income = float(input('What is the gross income of the year? '))

# Determine the tax based on income
if income <= 100000:
    # Apply a 1% tax rate for income up to $100,000
    tax = income * 0.01
elif income <= 500000:
    # Apply a 5% tax rate for income up to $500,000
    tax = income * 0.05
else:
    # Apply a 5% tax rate for the first $500,000
    # and a 2% tax rate for the amount above $500,000
    tax = 500000 * 0.05 + 0.02 * (income - 500000)

# Print the calculated tax, formatted to 2 decimal places
print(f'The tax is {tax:.2f}')
```

```
What is the gross income of year? 600000
The tax is 27000.00
```

7.4.3 A simple calculator

You are going to program a super simple Calculator.

Step1: Ask the user to enter the first number, store it in x

Step2: Ask the user to enter the second number, store it in y

Step3: Ask the user to enter the operator, store it in p

Step4: Calculate the result of x p y.

For example, if the user entered 2, 3, and +, you should print $2.0 + 3.0 = 5.0$ on the screen

```python
# Prompt the user to enter the first number and convert it to a float
x = float(input('Enter the first number: '))

# Prompt the user to enter the second number and convert it to a float
y = float(input('Enter the second number: '))

# Prompt the user to enter an operator (+, -, *, or /)
operator = input('Please enter the operator (one of +, -, *, /): ')

# Perform the operation based on the entered operator
if operator == '+':
    # If the operator is '+', perform addition and print the result
    print(x, operator, y, '=', x + y)
elif operator == '-':
```

```
  # If the operator is '-', perform subtraction and print the result
  print(x, operator, y, '=', x - y)
elif operator == '*':
  # If the operator is '*', perform multiplication and print the result
  print(x, operator, y, '=', x * y)
elif operator == '/':
  # If the operator is '/', perform division and print the result
  # Check for division by zero
  if y != 0:
    print(x, operator, y, '=', x / y)
  else:
    print("Error: Division by zero is not allowed")
```

```
Enter the first number: 3
Enter the second number: 4
Please enter the operator (one of +, -, *, /)+
3.0 + 4.0 = 7.0
```

7.4.4   Taxi fare calculator

You are going to program a simple Calculator for a taxi.

Step1: Ask the driver to enter total miles, store it in `miles`

Step2: Calculate the fare based on the formula

- if `miles` < 10, fare is $5.
- if 10 <= `miles` < 20, fare is $5 plus $1 for every mile beyond 10.
- if `miles` > 20, fare is $15 plus $1.5 for every mile beyond 20.

Step3: print the fare.

```
# Prompt the user to enter the total miles and convert it to a float
miles = float(input('Enter the total miles: '))

# Determine the fare based on the number of miles
if miles < 10:
  # Miles are less than 10, flat rate of $5
  fare = 5
elif miles < 20:
  # Miles are between 10 and 20, $5 + $1 per mile
  fare = 5 + (miles - 10)
else:
  # Miles are 20 or more, $15 + $1.50 per mile
  fare = 15 + 1.5 * (miles - 20)

# Print the calculated fare
print('The fare is:', fare)
```

```
Enter the total miles: 25
The fare is: 22.5
```

7.5 INTERACT WITH GENAI

Here are some questions and prompts you can interact with generative AI tools, including ChatGPT.

- What is branching in Python, and why is it important for controlling program flow?
- Explain how optional branching (`if`) works in Python. Provide a basic example.
- What is alternative branching (`if-else`), and how does it differ from optional branching?
- Describe multiple branching using `if-elif-else` and its use cases.
- What is the significance of indentation in Python branching statements?
- Show how to use multiple conditions in a single `if` statement with logical operators.
- Write an example that uses nested `if-else` statements to check multiple conditions.
- How does Python decide which block to execute in an `if-elif-else` structure?
- Can `if-else` statements be used without logical operators? Provide an example.
- What are potential pitfalls of using too many nested `if` statements? How can they be avoided?
- How do you handle cases where branching logic needs to evaluate complex conditions involving multiple variables?
- Write a program to determine if a year is a leap year using `if-else`.
- Create a menu-driven program where the user selects an option, and the program executes the corresponding action.
- How can you handle cases where multiple `if` statements conflict or overlap?
- What should you do if an `if-elif-else` structure does not cover all possible cases?

## CHAPTER 8

Repetition

REPETITION flow control lets us repeat a piece of code multiple times. This is done using loops, like `for` loops and `while` loops. Repetition is important because it saves our time and effort. Instead of writing the same code again and again, we can use loops to automate tasks. In real life, repetition is useful for things like processing all rows in a dataset, sending automated emails, or simulating events like rolling a dice many times. It makes coding more efficient and helps solve problems faster.

Let's get started!

8.1 CONDITION-BASED REPETITION

8.1.1 Explanation

In Python, condition-based repetition flow control is managed using the `while` loop. The `while` loop repeatedly executes a block of code as long as a specified condition remains true. This type of loop is ideal when you don't know beforehand how many times the loop should run, but you want the iteration to continue until a certain condition is no longer met.

Here's a basic structure of a `while` loop:

```
while condition:
    statements
```

Here, the loop checks this `condition` before each iteration. If the `condition` is `True`, the code block inside the loop will execute. If the `condition` is `False`, the loop stops and the program continues with the next lines of code outside the loop. The `statements` with indentation is the section of code that runs on each iteration while the `condition` is `True` (Figure 8.1).

DOI: 10.1201/9781003527725-8

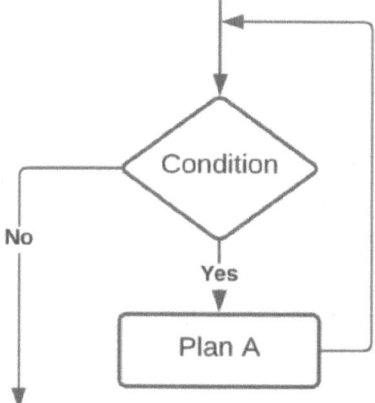

Figure 8.1 A flow chart for condition-based repetition.

8.1.2 Demonstration

```python
# Initialize a counter variable i to 0
i = 0

# Start a while loop that continues as long as i is less than 5
while i < 5:  # loop will run at most 5 times
    # Print the current value of i and a message
    print(f'i is {i}, the condition {i}<5 is satisfied. Keep going!')

    # Increment i by 1 at the end of each loop iteration
    i += 1

# Print a message indicating the loop has finished executing
print('The loop has terminated.')
```

```
i is 0, the condition 0<5 is satisfied. Keep going!
i is 1, the condition 1<5 is satisfied. Keep going!
i is 2, the condition 2<5 is satisfied. Keep going!
i is 3, the condition 3<5 is satisfied. Keep going!
i is 4, the condition 4<5 is satisfied. Keep going!
The loop has terminated.
```

```python
# Initialize a flag variable to True, which will control the loop
flag = True

# Start a while loop that continues as long as the flag is True
while flag:
    # Print a message indicating the current state of the flag
    print(f'The condition is {flag}. Keep going!')

    # Ask the user to enter a number and convert it to float
    # Check if the entered number is greater than 10
    # If yes, flag becomes False, otherwise it stays True
    num = float(input('Enter a number larger than 10: '))
    flag = num > 10
```

```
# If the number is not greater than 10, print an error message
if not flag:
  print('Error: Number is not larger than 10.')
```

```
The condition is True. Keep going!
Enter a number larger than 10: 11
The condition is True. Keep going!
Enter a number larger than 10: 12
The condition is True. Keep going!
Enter a number larger than 10: 10.01
The condition is True. Keep going!
Enter a number larger than 10: 10
Error: Number is not larger than 10.
```

8.1.3 Practice

Task: Print all integers from −5 to 5.

```
count = -5
while count <= 5:
  print(count)
  count += 1
```

```
-5
-4
-3
-2
-1
0
1
2
3
4
5
```

Task: Print all integers of an interval given by the user. Ask the user to enter two integers and print all integers between (including) them.

```
low = int(input('Enter the lower bound of interval: '))
high = int(input('Enter the upper bound of interval: '))
count = low
while count <= high:
  print(count)
  count += 1
```

```
Enter the lower bound of interval: 2
Enter the upper bound of interval: 5
2
3
4
5
```

Task: Double the Number.

1. Ask the user to enter a small positive number (0–10)
2. Double the number, print it out, and repeat, until the number beyond 1,000,000

```
n = int(input('Enter a small positive number (0-10): '))
while n <= 1000000:
  print(n)
  n *= 2 # n = n * 2
```

```
Enter a small positive number (0-10): 2
2
4
8
16
32
64
128
256
512
1024
2048
4096
8192
16384
32768
65536
131072
262144
524288
```

Task: Keep asking for candy until `'Done'`.

1. Ask the user to enter anything
2. Print a message `'Thanks! I got a candy'`
3. Repeat Steps 1 and 2, until the user enters `'Done'`
4. Print a message `'Thanks! I have enough'`

```
msg = input('Enter anything to continue, enter "Done" to stop: ')
while msg != 'Done':
  print('Thanks! I got a candy')
  msg = input('Enter anything to continue, enter "Done" to stop: ')
print('Thanks! I have enough')
```

```
Enter anything to continue, enter "Done" to stop: else
Thanks! I got a candy
Enter anything to continue, enter "Done" to stop: ok
Thanks! I got a candy
Enter anything to continue, enter "Done" to stop: Done
Thanks! I have enough
```

Task: Password setup

1. Ask the user to enter a new password.
2. Ask the user to enter the password again.
3. If the second input matches the first one, print "You are all set"; otherwise, repeat the process.

```
password1 = input('Enter a new password:')
password2 = input('Enter the password again:')
while password1 != password2:
  password1 = input('Enter a new password:')
  password2 = input('Enter the password again:')
print('You are all set')
```

```
Enter a new password:12
Enter the password again:3
Enter a new password:12
Enter the password again:12
You are all set
```

8.2 COUNT-BASED REPETITION

8.2.1 Explanation

In Python, count-based repetition flow control is managed using the `for` loop. The `for` loop iterates over a sequence (like a list, tuple, or range) and executes a block of code for each item in the sequence. It's ideal when you know in advance how many times you want to iterate.

Here's a basic structure of a `for` loop:

```
for item in sequence:
  statements
```

Here, the `item` represents the current element from the `sequence` that the loop is iterating over. The `sequence` can be any iterable, such as a list, tuple, string, or range. The loop will iterate once for each element in the `sequence`. The `statements` with indentation is the section of code that runs on each iteration (Figure 8.2).

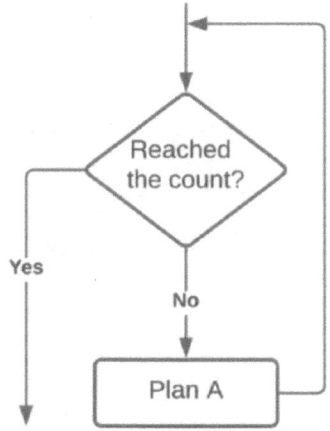

Figure 8.2 A flow chart for count-based repetition.

8.2.2   Demonstration

```
# Iterate over a list of numbers using a for loop
for i in [0, 1, 2, 3]:
  # Print the current number in the list
  print(i)
```

```
0
1
2
3
```

```
for i in [0, 1, 2, 3]:
  print('Hello, world')
```

```
Hello, world
Hello, world
Hello, world
Hello, world
```

```
for i in range(3):
  print(i, 'Hello, world!')
```

```
0 Hello, world!
1 Hello, world!
2 Hello, world!
```

```
for i in range(5):
  print(i)
```

```
0
1
2
3
4
```

```
for i in range(0, 5):
  print(i)
```

```
0
1
2
3
4
```

```
for i in range(2, 5):
  print(i)
```

```
2
3
4
```

```
for i in range(2, 5, 1):
  print(i)
```

```
2
3
```

4

```
for i in range(2, 5, 2):
  print(i)
```

2
4

8.2.3 Practice

Task: Print all even numbers within 20

```
for i in range(21):
  if i % 2 == 0:
    print(i)
```

0
2
4
6
8
10
12
14
16
18
20

```
for i in range(0, 21, 2):
  print(i)
```

0
2
4
6
8
10
12
14
16
18
20

Task: Print all numbers dividable by 5 within 100

```
for i in range(101):
  if i % 5 == 0:
    print(i)
```

0
5
10
15
20
25
30

```
35
40
45
50
55
60
65
70
75
80
85
90
95
100
```

```
for i in range(0, 101, 5):
  print(i)
```

```
0
5
10
15
20
25
30
35
40
45
50
55
60
65
70
75
80
85
90
95
100
```

Task: Print all integers from –5 to 5.

```
for i in range(-5, 6):
  print(i)
```

```
-5
-4
-3
-2
-1
0
1
2
3
4
5
```

Task: Print all integers of an interval given by the user. Ask the user to enter two integers and print all integers between (including) them.

```python
low = int(input('Enter the lower bound of the interval: '))
high = int(input('Enter the higher bound of the interval: '))
for i in range(low, high+1):
  print(i)
```

```
Enter the lower bound of the interval: 2
Enter the higher bound of the interval: 5
2
3
4
5
```

8.3 MAGIC CONTROL

In Python, `break` and `continue` are flow control statements that allow you to skip or exit loops based on certain conditions. The `break` statement immediately exits the loop, stopping further iterations, while the `continue` statement skips the current iteration and moves to the next one.

In both `for` and `while` loops, `break` can be used to stop the loop early, and `continue` can be used to skip the remaining part of the loop's body for that iteration.

8.3.1 Demonstration

```python
# Initialize a win condition to False, which will control the loop
win = False

# Start a while loop that continues as long as win is False
while not win:
  # Set the magic number to 5
  magic = 5

  # Ask the user to guess an integer or quit
  x = input('Guess an integer in 0-10, "exit" to leave: ')

  # Check if the user wants to exit
  if x.upper() == 'EXIT':
    # Print a farewell message and break out of the loop
    print(f'Sorry to see you go!')
    break

  # Check if the user's guess is outside the valid range
  if int(x) < 0 or int(x) > 10:
    # Print a hint and continue to the next iteration
    print(f'You are still far! Do it again')
    continue

  # Check if the user's guess is not equal to the magic number
  elif int(x) != magic:
    # Print a hint and continue to the next iteration
```

```
    print(f'You are close! Do it again!')
    continue

# Print a success message and set win to True
print(f'You got it! The magic number is {magic}!')
win = True
```

```
Guess an integer in 0-10, "exit" to leave: 12
You are still far! Do it again
Guess an integer in 0-10, "exit" to leave: 10
You are close! Do it again!
Guess an integer in 0-10, "exit" to leave: 8
You are close! Do it again!
Guess an integer in 0-10, "exit" to leave: 3
You are close! Do it again!
Guess an integer in 0-10, "exit" to leave: 5
You got it! The magic number is 5!
```

8.3.2 Practice

Task: Check each integer in **range(1, 20)**, if the number is divisible by 5, skip the iteration and turn to next one; otherwise, print it out.

```
for i in range(1, 20):
  if i %5 == 0:
    continue
  print(i)
```

```
1
2
3
4
6
7
8
9
11
12
13
14
16
17
18
19
```

Task: Check each integer in **range(1, 20)**, if the number is divisible by 5, stop the iteration immediately; otherwise, print it out.

```
for i in range(1, 20):
  if i %5 == 0:
    break
  print(i)
```

```
1
2
3
```

4

8.4 CASE STUDIES OF REPETITION

These case studies are designed to test your understanding of flow control: repetition. We are going to create some simple programs using these tools. Are you ready? Let's get started!

You will find some real-life tasks in the sections below. You should use input() to get the user to enter the information and use print() to print the information on the screen. At this moment, we can assume users will follow instructions carefully – they will enter the valid inputs as required.

8.4.1 Prime numbers

1. Ask the user to enter an integer.
2. Find and print all prime numbers up to the integer.

```python
# Ask the user to enter an integer
n = int(input('Enter an integer: '))

# Start a loop that iterates from 2 to n (inclusive)
for i in range(2, n+1):
    # Assume i is prime
    prime = True

    # Check if i has any divisors other than 1 and itself
    for j in range(2, i):
        # If the i is divisible by any other number, it's not prime
        if i % j == 0:
            prime = False
            # Break out of the inner loop since i is not prime
            break

    # If the current number is prime, print it
    if prime:
        print(i)
```

```
Enter an integer: 20
2
3
5
7
11
13
17
19
```

8.4.2 A simple grade book

1. Ask the user to enter the number of students in a class.
2. Ask the user to enter the grade (on a 0–100 scale) of each student.

3. Calculate and print the average, min, and max grades of the class.

```python
# Ask the user to enter the number of students
n = int(input('Enter the number of students: '))

# Initialize variables
total = 0  # Initialize total as 0
min = 100  # Initialize min with a high value
max = 0  # Initialize max with a low value

# Start a loop to iterate over each student
for i in range(n):
    # Ask the user to enter the grade of the current student
    grade = int(input('Enter the grade of the student: '))

    # Add the current grade to the total
    total += grade

    # Update the minimum grade if the current grade is lower
    if grade < min:
        min = grade

    # Update the maximum grade if the current grade is higher
    if grade > max:
        max = grade

# Calculate the average grade and print the results
print(f'Average: {total/n:.2f}. Min: {min}. Max: {max}')
```

```
Enter the number of students: 3
Enter the grade of the student: 100
Enter the grade of the student: 99
Enter the grade of the student: 90
Average: 96.33. Min: 90. Max:100
```

8.4.3 Fahrenheit to Celsius converter

1. Ask the user to enter the number in Fahrenheit (enter stop to quit the program)
2. Calculate the Celsius based on the formular c = (f – 32) * 5 / 9
3. Print the Celsius

```python
# Ask the user to enter a temperature in Fahrenheit or quit
f = input('Enter the Fahrenheit (enter "stop" to quit): ')

# Start a loop that continues until the user types "stop"
while f != 'stop':
    # Convert the user's input to a floating-point number
    f = float(f)

    # Convert the Fahrenheit temperature to Celsius
    c = (f - 32) * 5 / 9

    # Print the result, rounding to the nearest whole number
    print(f'Celsius is {c:.0f}')
```

```
# Ask the user to enter another temperature or quit
f = input('Enter the Fahrenheit (enter "stop" to quit): ')
```

```
Enter the Fahrenheit (enter "stop" to quit): 32
Celsius is 0
Enter the Fahrenheit (enter "stop" to quit): 98
Celsius is 37
Enter the Fahrenheit (enter "stop" to quit): 24
Celsius is -4
Enter the Fahrenheit (enter "stop" to quit): stop
```

8.4.4   How many E and e are in a sentence?

1. Ask the user to enter a sentence
2. Count the number of `'E'` and the number of `'e'` in the sentence
3. Print the result

```
# Ask the user to enter a sentence
sentence = input('Enter a sentence: ')

# Initialize counters for lowercase 'e' and uppercase 'E'
number_e = 0
number_E = 0

# Iterate over each character in the sentence
for c in sentence:
  # If the character is lowercase 'e', increment the counter
  if c == 'e':
    number_e += 1
  # If the character is uppercase 'E', increment the counter
  elif c == 'E':
    number_E += 1

# Print the total counts of 'e' and 'E'
print(f'Number of e: {number_e}. Number of E: {number_E}.')
```

```
Enter a sentence: Example Sentence with EeeeEEEEE
Number of e: 7. Number of E: 7.
```

8.5   INTERACT WITH GENAI

Here are some questions and prompts you can interact with generative AI tools, including ChatGPT.

- How does a `for` loop work? What types of sequences can it iterate over?
- What is the purpose of the `break` statement in loops? Provide an example.
- Describe the use of the `continue` statement in loops.
- What are infinite loops, and how can you prevent them when using `while` loops?
- Can a `for` loop iterate over a string? If so, what will it do?
- How does the loop counter in a `for` loop behave when the `range()` is used?
- How do you implement a nested loop to process multi-dimensional data (e.g., a list of lists)?

- What should you do if a loop is running indefinitely and you need to debug it?
- Why might the `break` statement not exit a loop as expected? How can you resolve this?
- What are common causes of skipping iterations unintentionally in loops? How can you fix them?
- How do you avoid nested loops becoming too complex or slow in execution?

Functions

L ET us learn something even more powerful than branching and repetition. Imagine you want to jump to a different place, do something, then return to the place you started? It feels like traversing multiple universes, as depicted in the movie *Everything Everywhere All at Once*! You can do it, with functions! In this chapter, we are going to learn how to call functions and then how to define various functions, from the basic to complex ones. You'll unlock more power of Python.

Are you ready? Let's get started!

9.1 WHAT ARE FUNCTIONS?

9.1.1 Explanation

Functions are the building blocks of reusable code in Python. They allow us to group related code into logical units, making our programs more organized, readable, and maintainable. Think of functions as self-contained recipes that can be executed multiple times with different inputs, resulting in consistent and efficient code (Figure 9.1).

Functions serve several purposes: 1) Write the code once, and use it many times throughout your program, 2) Divide your code into smaller, manageable chunks, making it easier to maintain and debug, and 3) Organize your code into logical sections, making it easier for others (or yourself) to understand.

Functions may hide the implementation details of a task from the rest of your program, allowing you to focus on the interface (inputs/outputs) rather than the internal workings. Functions reduce duplicated code and make your program more maintainable and minimize the amount of code you need to write and execute. You can easily modify or extend functions without affecting the rest of your program.

DOI: 10.1201/9781003527725-9

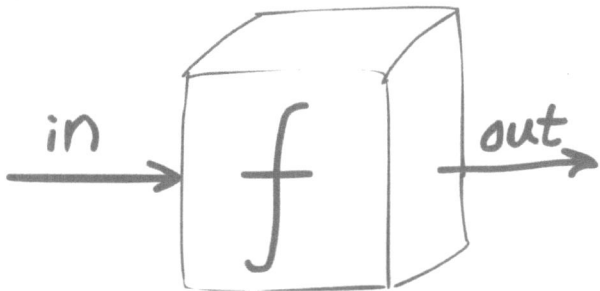

Figure 9.1   A function as a box.

9.1.2   Example: Bread toaster

Imagine you want to toast some bread. You don't need to learn how to build a toaster from scratch; instead, you can buy a pre-built toaster that takes bread (input) as an argument and produces toasted bread (output). The internal workings of the toaster are abstracted away, making it easy for anyone to use.

Similarly, in Python, functions work like a black box. You pass inputs (arguments) into the function, and it returns a specific output or result. You don't need to know how the function works internally; you just need to understand its interface (inputs/outputs).

Of course, you can design your own function and provide its functionality for other people to use – that is how the community of Python is doing. Everyone contributes and every benefits!

9.1.3   Practice

Task: Think about some examples in your real life, the function-like things, and describe them as input-process-output (IPO) flow.

Task: Describe the following functions in the IPO style:

```
print(value)
input(prompt)
str(value)
int(value)
range(5)
range(2, 10, 3)
```

Task: Apply `help(function)` to get more insights into the `function`, for example, `help(print)`

```
help(print)
```

```
Help on built-in function print in module builtins:

print(...)
    print(value, ..., sep=' ', end='\n', file=sys.stdout, flush=False)

    Prints the values to a stream, or to sys.stdout by default.
```

```
Optional keyword arguments:
file:  a file-like object (stream); defaults to the current sys.stdout.
sep:   string inserted between values, default a space.
end:   string appended after the last value, default a newline.
flush: whether to forcibly flush the stream.
```

9.2 TYPES OF FUNCTIONS

9.2.1 Explanation

Depending on whether or not a function has return values, we group functions into two categories:

1. Functions with no return values: A function with no return value is simply a procedure that performs an action and doesn't produce any output.
2. Functions with return values: A function with return value(s) is able to pass the value to a variable or another function for further process.

Depending on the number of parameters, we group functions into three categories:

1. Functions with no parameters
2. Functions with one parameter
3. Functions with two or more parameters

9.3 DEFINE A FUNCTION

Let's start with simple ones: functions without parameters.

9.3.1 Demonstration

```
def say_hello():
  print('Hello!')

say_hello()  # Output: Hello!
```

```
Hello!
```

Here, the definition of a function starts with the keyword `def`, followed by the name of the function, `say_hello`, with a pair of parenthesis `()`. The `:` indicates the end of definition clause and leads to the actual definitions, the statements of the function, which will have an indentation as we learned in branching and repetition structures. In this instance, the statement is simply to print a string out. The `say_hello()` function doesn't require any inputs since there is no parameter in the `()`. When we call it, it simply prints the greeting to the console.

```
def say_goodbye():
  for i in range(3):
    print(f'Goodbye, Py')

say_goodbye()  # Output: Goodbye, Py! three times
```

```
Goodbye, Py
Goodbye, Py
Goodbye, Py
```

This example defines a function say_goodbye() that prints the message 'Goodbye, Py!' 3 times.

```
def empty():
  pass

empty()
```

The example defines a function empty() that has empty content. We may use this function as a placeholder and complete it later on.

9.3.2 Practice

Task: Define a function hello_world() that prints 'hello world'.

```
def hello_world():
  print('Hello, world')

hello_world()
```

```
Hello, world
```

Task: Define a function hello_world() that prints 'hello world' three times.

```
def hello_world_3():
  for i in range(3):
    print('Hello, world')

hello_world_3()
```

```
Hello, world
Hello, world
Hello, world
```

Task: Define a function print1to10() that prints integer 1, 2, ..., 10 (hint: you can use a for loop).

```
def print1to10():
  for i in range(1, 11):
    print(i)

print1to10()
```

```
1
2
3
4
5
6
7
8
```

9
10

Task: Define a function `prime_in_100()` that prints primary integers in 100 (hint: you can use loops).

```python
def prime_in_100():
  for i in range(2, 100):
    prime = True
    for j in range(2, i):
      if i % j == 0:
        prime = False
        break
    if prime:
      print(i)

prime_in_100()
```

2
3
5
7
11
13
17
19
23
29
31
37
41
43
47
53
59
61
67
71
73
79
83
89
97

Task: Define a function `even_in_10()` that prints even number from 1 to 10.

```python
def even_in_10():
  for i in range(1, 11):
    if i % 2 == 0:
      print(i)

even_in_10()
```

2
4
6

8
10

Task: Define a function `odd_in_10()` that prints odd number from 1 to 10.

```python
def odd_in_10():
  for i in range(1, 11):
    if i % 2 != 0:
      print(i)

odd_in_10()
```

1
3
5
7
9

Task: Define a function `print_welcome()` that prints `'Welcome, {your name}!'` where `your name` is received from the user.

```python
def print_welcome():
  print(f'Welcome, {input("What is your name? ")}!')

print_welcome()
```

What is your name? Neo
Welcome, Neo!

9.4   PARAMETERS AND ARGUMENTS

9.4.1   Explanation

Before we learn how to define functions with one parameter, let's clarify parameters and arguments. A parameter is a variable defined within a function that takes on a value passed to it when the function is called. Think of it as an input slot for your function that accepts values. An argument, on the other hand, is the actual value provided to a function when it's called. It's what fills up that input slot or parameter. A function with one parameter performs an action that may or may not use the input value passed to it when called.

9.4.2   Demonstration

```python
def greet(name):
  print(f'Hello, {name}!')
greet('Alice')   # Output: Hello, Alice!
```

Hello, Alice!

Here, `name` is a parameter defined in the `greet` function, and `'Alice'` is an argument passed to the function when we call it. You can imagine the step-by-step function as:

```python
greet('Alice')
# search for greet(name) function
```

```
# found greet(name) function definition, go there
name = 'Alice'
print(f'Hello, Alice!')
# return to where greet('Alice') was called
```

As you can see from the above step-by-step process, when you pass an argument to a function, you're assigning the value of argument to the parameter. This is called passing by value.

```
def double(x):
    x = x * 2
    print(f'x is {x}.')  # output: 10

a = 5
double(a)
print(f'a is {a}')   # Output: 5
```

```
x is 10.
a is 5
```

In this example, a refers to 5. When we pass a to the function double(x), actually, 5 is passed to x, which is doubled in the function. Thus, we have x as 10 and a as 5.

9.4.3 Practice

Task: Define a function hello_name(name) that prints 'hello, {name}' where name is a parameter.

```
def hello_name(name):
    print('hello,', name)

hello_name('Di')
```

```
hello, Di
```

Task: Define a function hello_world_n(n) that prints 'hello world' n times, where n is a parameter.

```
def hello_world_n(n):
    for i in range(n):
        print('hello world')

hello_world_n(3)
```

```
hello world
hello world
hello world
```

Task: Define a function print_int_1_n(n) that prints integers 1 to n (hint: you can use a for loop), where n is a parameter.

```
def print_int_1_n(n):
    for i in range(n):
        print(i + 1)
```

```
print_int_1_n(10)
```

```
1
2
3
4
5
6
7
8
9
10
```

Task: Define a function `print_prime_2_n(n)` that prints all prime integers in `[2, n]` (hint: you can use loops), where `n` is a parameter.

```
def print_prime_2_n(n):
  for i in range(2, n+1):
    prime = True
    for j in range(2, i):
      if i % j == 0:
        prime = False
        break
    if prime:
      print(i)

print_prime_1_n(10)
```

```
2
3
5
7
```

Task: Define a function `even(n)` that prints whether or not given `n` is even, `n` is a parameter.

```
def even(n):
  if n % 2 == 0:
    print(n,'is even')
  else:
    print(n,'is not even')

even(1)
even(2)
```

```
1 is not even
2 is even
```

Task: Define a function `abs(n)` that prints the absolute value of `n`, `n` is a parameter.

```
def abs(n):
  if n < 0:
    n = -n
  print(n)
```

```
abs(-1)
abs(1)
```

```
1
1
```

Task: Define a function `square(n)` that prints the square value of n, n is a parameter.

```
def square(n):
    print(n * n)

square(2)
square(3)
```

```
4
9
```

Task: Define a function `divisible_by_6(n)` that prints whether or not given n is divisible by 6, n is a parameter.

```
def divisible_by_6(n):
    if n % 6 == 0:
        print(n, 'is divisible by 6')
    else:
        print(n, 'is not divisible by 6')
```

Task: Define a function `prime(n)` that prints whether or not given n is a prime number, n is a parameter.

```
def prime(n):
    prime = True
    for i in range(2, n):
        if n % i == 0:
            prime = False
            break
    if prime:
        print(n, 'is prime')
    else:
        print(n, 'is not prime')

prime(3)
prime(4)
```

```
3 is prime
4 is not prime
```

9.5 TWO PARAMETERS

Functions with two parameters are just as straightforward as their single-parameter counterparts. Each parameter has its own role to play within the function, allowing you to perform more complex operations or calculations.

A function with two parameters takes in not one, but two arguments when called.

9.5.1 Demonstration

```
def rectangle_area(length, width):
  return length * width
print(rectangle_area(4.5, 6))  # Output: 27.0
```

27.0

```
def sum(a, b):
  return a + b

print(sum(5, 10))   # Output: 15
```

15

```
def average(a, b):
  return (a + b) / 2

print(average(20, 30))   # Output: 25.0
```

25.0

9.5.2 Practice

Task: Define a function print_message_n(message, n) that prints message n times, where message and n are parameters.

```
def print_message_n(message, n):
  for i in range(n):
    print(message)

print_message_n('Hello, world!', 3)
```

```
Hello, world!
Hello, world!
Hello, world!
```

Task: Define a function print_n_to_m(n, m) that prints integers n to m (hint: you can use a for loop), where n and m are parameters and n < m.

Challenge: Can you write a program print_n_to_m_challenge(n, m) that doesn't require n < m?

```
def print_n_to_m(n, m):
  for i in range(n, m+1):
    print(i)

print_n_to_m(2, 5)
```

```
2
3
4
5
```

```python
def print_n_to_m_challenge(n, m):
  if n <= m:
    for i in range(n, m+1):
      print(i)
  else:
    for i in range(n, m-1, -1):
      print(i)

print_n_to_m_challenge(2, 5)
print_n_to_m_challenge(5, 2)
```

```
2
3
4
5
5
4
3
2
```

Task: Define a function `sum_n_to_m(n, m)` that prints the total of integers n to m, where n and m are parameters, and n < m.

```python
def sum_n_to_m(n, m):
  sum = 0
  for i in range(n, m+1):
    sum += i
  print(sum)

sum_n_to_m(2, 5)
```

```
14
```

Task: Define a function `and_operation(condition1, condition2)` that prints the `and` logical operation of `condition1` and `condition2`, where `condition1`, `condition2` are parameters.

```python
def and_operation(condition1, condition2):
  print(condition1 and condition2)

and_operation(True, True)
and_operation(True, False)
```

```
True
False
```

Task: Define a function `n_divisible_m(n, m)` that prints if integer n is divisible by integer m, where n and m are parameters.

```python
def n_divisible_m(n, m):
  if n % m == 0:
    print(n, 'is divisible by', m)
  else:
    print(n, 'is not divisible by', m)
```

```
n_divisible_m(3, 2)

n_divisible_m(4, 2)
```

```
3 is not divisible by 2
4 is divisible by 2
```

Task: Define a function `min(x, y, z)` that prints the minimal number among integers x, y, and z, where x, y, and z are parameters

```
def min(x, y, z):
    min = x
    if y < min:
        min = y
    if z < min:
        min = z
    print(min)

min(1, 2, 3)
min(6, 5, 4)
```

```
1
4
```

Task: Define a function `speed(distance, time)` that takes the `distance` and `time` as inputs and prints the speed as `distance/time`.

```
def average_speed(distance, time):
    print(distance / time)

print(average_speed(10, 3))
```

9.6   HOW TO PASS ARGUMENTS

In Python, when defining a function with multiple parameters, there are two ways to pass these parameters: by position and by keyword. Let's explore the advantages and disadvantages of each method.

9.6.1   Demonstration

```
def greet(name, age):
    print(f'Hello, {name}! You are {age} years old.')

greet('Neo', 18)  # Output: Hello, Neo! You are 18 years old.
```

```
Hello, Neo! You are 18 years old.
```

```
greet(18, 'Neo') # It will print a meaningless message.
```

```
Hello, 18! You are Neo years old.
```

In above-mentioned example, we passed arguments by position, so that `'Neo'` was assigned to `name` and 18 was assigned to `age`. It is easy to use. You don't need to remember the parameter names and you only need to provide values in the correct order. However, if you accidentally swap the argument positions, it will result in incorrect behavior. If there are many parameters, this approach can become confusing, especially when calling the function. Let's try passing by keywords then.

```
greet(age=18, name='Neo')  # Output: Hello, Neo! You are 18 years old
```

```
Hello, Neo! You are 18 years old.
```

```
greet(name='Neo', age=18)  # Output: Hello, Neo! You are 18 years old
```

```
Hello, Neo! You are 18 years old.
```

In above-mentioned two examples, we passed arguments by keywords, so that `'Neo'` was explicitly assigned to `name`, and `18` was explicitly assigned to `age`. There is no confusion anymore. Keyword arguments make the code more readable by clearly indicating which parameter is being set. You can pass keyword arguments in any order because they are explicitly named. However, you need to use the exact name of the parameter when passing a value. This approach requires more effort to understand the code, especially for complex functions with many parameters.

In conclusion, if you're working with a small number of well-known function arguments and don't mind using position-based arguments, go with positional arguments. For larger or more complex function signatures with multiple optional arguments, use keyword arguments. This approach can help reduce errors and improve readability. This is the more common scenario when we use Python for data science.

9.6.2 Practice

Task: Call functions you defined in previous practice, passing arguments by keywords, and experience the difference.

9.7 DEFAULT VALUE

In Python, you can assign a default value to a function parameter when defining it. This allows for more flexibility and convenience when calling the function.

9.7.1 Demonstration

```
def greet(name, msg='Hi'):
  print(f'{msg}, {name}!')

greet('Neo')  # Output: Hi, Neo!
```

```
Hi, Neo!
```

In the `greet()` function definition, we provided the default values for `msg` parameter as `'Hi'`. This means that if we don't pass any value for `msg` when calling the function, it will take on the default values. Please note that the parameters with default values must be after the parameters without default values; in this example, `msg` must be after `name` since `name` has no default value.

By assigning default values to some parameters, you make them optional, which is especially useful for functions with a large number of arguments. When calling a function, you can skip passing values for optional parameters if the defaults work. The use of default values can clarify what these arguments are supposed to do or how they might be used. However, it's important to ensure that you're not creating overlapping functionality by having multiple possible input scenarios. Also, make sure to document the purpose and expected behavior of optional parameters well, so others (or yourself) understand what they do in different contexts.

```python
greet('Neo', 'Hello')  # Hello, Neo!
```

```
Hello, Neo!
```

```python
def print_numbers(end, start=0, step=1):
  while start < end:
    print(start)
    start += step
```

```python
print_numbers(5)
```

```
0
1
2
3
4
```

```python
print_numbers(start = 2, end = 5)
```

```
2
3
4
```

```python
print_numbers(start = 2, end = 5, step = 2)
```

```
2
4
```

Now we can understand the `print()` and `range()` better, since they have defined default parameters that provide optional customizations when needed.

9.7.2 Practice

Task: Define a function called `sum_of_squares` that takes two numbers, `a` and `b`, as inputs and prints the sum of their squares. If no value is provided for either argument, then `a` should default to 1, and `b` should default to 2.

```python
# Define a function to calculate the sum of squares of two numbers
def sum_of_squares(a=1, b=2):
  # Print the sum of squares of a and b
  print(a ** 2 + b ** 2)

# Call the function with default arguments (a=1, b=2)
sum_of_squares()            # output: 5
```

```
# Call the function with a=2 and default b=2
sum_of_squares(a=2)          # output: 8

# Call the function with default a=1 and b=3
sum_of_squares(b=3)          # output: 10

# Call the function with both a=3 and b=4
sum_of_squares(a=3, b=4)     # output: 25
```

```
5
8
10
25
```

Task: Define a function `welcome()` that takes two arguments `start_time` (default value as '17:30') and `verb` (default value as 'start'). The program can:

1. Convert the `start_time` to minutes from 0:00 of the day, and save it to `start`.
2. Ask the user to enter the current time in 24-hour `hh:mm` format, such as `17:05`, and convert it to minutes from 0:00 of the day, and save it to `current`.
3. Calculate how many minutes are left by comparing the minutes of current time and the minutes of the start_time, and save it to `left`.
4. Print a message `'Welcome to our class! We will {verb} in {left} minutes!'`
5. Keep above steps until the left is less than 1.

```
# Define a function to welcome students to a class
def welcome(start_time='17:30', verb='start'):
  # Convert the start time from 'hh:mm' format to minutes
  start = 60 * int(start_time[:2]) + int(start_time[-2:])

  # Loop indefinitely until the break statement is reached
  while True:
    # Ask the user to enter the current time in 'hh:mm' format
    current = input('Enter current time in hh:mm format: ')

    # Convert the current time from 'hh:mm' format to minutes
    current = 60 * int(current[:2]) + int(current[-2:])

    # Calculate the time left until the class starts
    left = start - current

    # If the time left is less than 1 , break out of the loop
    if left < 1:
      break

    # Print a message with the time left until the class starts
    print(f'Welcome to our class! We will {verb} in {left} minutes!')
```

```
welcome()
```

```
Enter current time in hh:mm format: 17:05
Welcome to our class! We will start in 25 minutes!
Enter current time in hh:mm format: 17:25
```

```
Welcome to our class! We will start in 5 minutes!
Enter current time in hh:mm format: 17:30
```

```
welcome('19:00', 'resume')
```

```
Enter current time in hh:mm format: 18:55
Welcome to our class! We will resume in 5 minutes!
Enter current time in hh:mm format: 18:59
Welcome to our class! We will resume in 1 minutes!
Enter current time in hh:mm format: 19:00
```

9.8 RETURN VALUES

Functions with return values are an essential part of coding and understanding how they work is crucial for writing effective code.

9.8.1 Explanation

What are return values? In Python, when a function completes its execution, it can return a value back to the calling program. This returned value is called the function's return value or simply the return. Think of a return value as the answer your function gives you after processing some input. The caller (the code that calls the function) receives this value and can use it as needed.

Functions with return values are reusable because they encapsulate logic, making it easy to integrate them into other parts of your program. Return values help you structure your code more effectively by allowing functions to perform a specific task and then share the results with other parts of your program. Using return values enables you to write more concise code because the result of a function call can be stored in a variable, reducing repetition.

When performing complex calculations, return values enable you to store the result and use it further in your program. Return values can be used to manipulate data structures, such as lists or dictionaries. Functions with return values are particularly useful when working with conditionals (if-else statements).

9.8.2 Demonstration

To define a function that returns a value, you simply include the **return** statement with the desired output. Here's an example:

```
def greet(name):
  return f'Hello, {name}!'
```

In this case, the **greet()** function takes a single argument (**name**) and returns a greeting message.

```
greet('Neo')
```

```
{"type":"string"}
```

```
print(greet('Neo'))
```

Hello, Neo!

9.9   RETURN NUMERIC VALUES

Return values can be int and float.

9.9.1   Demonstration

```
int(5.5)
```

5

```
float(5)
```

5.0

```
def give_me_5():
    return 5

give_me_5()
```

5

```
def give_me_float():
    return 5.0

give_me_float()
```

5.0

9.9.2   Practice

Task: Define a function abs(n) that returns the absolute value of n.

```
def abs(n):
    if n < 0:
        n = -n
    return n

print(abs(-1))
print(abs(1))
```

1
1

Task: Define a function product(n, m) that returns the product value of n and m.

```
def product(n, m):
    return n * m

print(product(2, 5))
print(product(3, 2))
```

10
6

Task: Define a function `power(n, m)` that returns the result of raising `n` to the power of `m`.

```
def power(n, m):
    return n ** m

print(power(2, 3))
print(power(3, 2))
```

8
9

Task: Define a function `average(x, y, z)` that returns the average of three numbers, x, y, and z.

```
def average(x, y, z):
    return (x + y + z) / 3

print(average(1, 2, 3))
print(average(6, 5, 4))
```

2.0
5.0

Task: Define a function `min(x, y, z)` that returns the minimal of three numbers x, y, and z.

```
def min(x, y, z):
    min = x
    if y < min:
        min = y
    if z < min:
        min = z
    return min

print(min(1, 2, 3))
print(min(6, 5, 4))
```

1
4

Task: Define a function `sum_n(n)` that returns the sum of integers 1 to n (hint: you can use a for loop).

```
def sum_n(n):
    sum = 0
    for i in range(1, n+1):
        sum += i
    return sum

print(sum_n(10))
print(sum_n(100))
```

```
55
5050
```

9.10 RETURN STR VALUES

Return values can be `str`.

9.10.1 Demonstration

```
str(5)
```

```
{"type":"string"}
```

```
def give_me_FIVE():
  return 'FIVE'

give_me_FIVE()
```

```
{"type":"string"}
```

9.10.2 Practice

Task: Define a function `welcome(name)` that returns `'Welcome, {name}!'`.

```
def welcome(name):
  return f'Welcome, {name}!'

print(welcome('Neo'))
print(welcome('Alice'))
```

```
Welcome, Neo!
Welcome, Alice!
```

Task: Define a function `concatenate(msg1, msg2)` that concatenates `msg1` and `msg2` together and returns it.

```
def concatenate(msg1, msg2):
  return msg1 + msg2

print(concatenate('hello, ','world!'))
```

```
hello, world!
```

9.11 RETURN BOOLEAN VALUES

Return values can be `bool`.

9.11.1 Demonstration

```
def give_me_True():
  return True

give_me_True()
```

True

9.11.2 Practice

Task: Define a function `even(n)` that returns the Boolean value for given n is even or not.

```
def even(n):
  if n % 2 == 0:
    return True
  else:
    return False

print(even(1))
print(even(2))
```

False
True

Task: Define a function `prime(n)` that returns the Boolean value for given n is prime number or not.

```
def prime(n):
  for i in range(2, n):
    if n % i == 0:
      return False
  return True

print(prime(3))
print(prime(4))
```

True
False

Task: Define a function `positive(n)` that returns the Boolean value for given n is positive (>0) or not.

```
def positive(n):
  return n > 0

print(positive(1))
print(positive(-1))
```

True
False

Task: Define a function `divisible_6(n)` that returns the Boolean value for whether or not given n is divisible by 6.

```
def divisible_6(n):
  if n % 6 == 0:
    return True
  return False
```

9.12   RETURN MULTIPLE VALUES

Return values can be multiple ones with various data types.

9.12.1   Demonstration

```
def get_profile():
  first = input('Enter your first name: ')
  last = input('Enter your last name: ')
  age = int(input('Enter your age: '))
  zip = input('Enter your zip code: ')
  return first, last, age, zip

print(get_profile())
```

```
Enter your first name: Thomas
Enter your last name: Anderson
Enter your age: 18
Enter your zip code: 09090
('Thomas', 'Anderson', 18, '09090')
```

9.12.2   Practice

Task: Define a function `stats(x, y, z)` that returns the min, max, avg, and total of given three numbers x, y, and z.

```
def stats(x, y, z):
  min = x
  max = x
  total = 0
  if y < min:
    min = y
  if y > max:
    max = y
  if z < min:
    min = z
  if z > max:
    max = z
  total = x + y + z
  return min, max, total/3, total

print(stats(1, 2, 3))
```

```
(1, 3, 2.0, 6)
```

Challenge: Define a function stats() that:

1. Ask the user how many numbers to be entered.
2. Let the user enter the numbers.

3. Print the statistics of the numbers entered.
4. Return the min, max, mean, and total.

A test run is as follows:

```
How many numbers you are going to enter? 3
Please enter the numbers you have 3 left: 2
Please enter the numbers you have 2 left: 3
Please enter the numbers you have 1 left: 4
Your entered three numbers 2.0 3.0 4.0
  The min is 2.0.
  The max is 4.0.
  The mean is 3.0.
  The total is 9.0.
```

```python
def stats():
  n = int(input('How many numbers you are going to enter? '))
  numbers = ''
  total = 0
  for i in range(n):
    number = float(input(f'Please enter the numbers, you have {n-i} left: '))
    if i == 0:
      min, max = number, number
    if number < min:
      min = number
    if number > max:
      max = number
    numbers += f'{number} '
    total += number
  print(f'''Your entered {n} numbers: {numbers}
The min is {min:.2f}.
The max is {max:.2f}.
The mean is {total/n:.2f}.
The total is {total:.2f}.
''')
  return min, max, total/n, total
```

```python
print(stats())
```

```
How many numbers you are going to enter? 5
Please enter the numbers  you have 5 left: 1.1
Please enter the numbers you have 4 left: 2.2
Please enter the numbers you have 3 left: 3.3
Please enter the numbers you have 2 left: -9
Please enter the numbers you have 1 left: 4.4
Your entered 5 numbers: 1.1 2.2 3.3 -9.0 4.4
  The min is -9.00.
  The max is 4.40.
  The mean is 0.40.
  The total is 2.00.

(-9.0, 4.4, 0.4, 2.0)
```

9.13   INTERACT WITH GENAI

Here are some questions and prompts you can interact with generative AI tools, including ChatGPT.

- What is a function in Python and the role it plays in programming? Why is it beneficial to use functions?
- Why are functions important for organizing code? How do functions help in making code more readable and maintainable?
- How do functions contribute to code reusability? Why is it better to write a function instead of repeating the same code multiple times?
- Provide an example of how a function can simplify a program by reducing redundancy. Show a scenario where a block of code is used multiple times and how converting it into a function can improve the program.
- Illustrate how functions can make complex programs easier to understand by breaking them down into smaller, more manageable parts.
- Design an exercise where you identify parts of a program that could be improved by using a function. Describe how a function could simplify the code.
- Explain how to define a function in Python that takes no parameters. What is the purpose of such a function?
- Discuss scenarios where you might want to use a function without parameters.
- Show how a function with no parameters can be used to do repetitive tasks.
- Write a function with no parameters that simulates rolling a die.
- Discuss the difference between position-based arguments and keyword arguments when calling a function. Why might you choose one over the other?
- Describe the use of default parameters in functions. How do default parameters make your functions more flexible?
- Explain how to define a function in Python that returns a value. What is the significance of the `return` statement in a function?
- Discuss how returning different data types from a function can be useful in various programming scenarios.
- Describe how a function can return multiple values at once. Why might it be beneficial to return multiple pieces of data from a single function?
- Generate an example of a Python function that returns a `str`, such as a function that takes a name as an argument and returns a greeting message.
- Provide an example of a function that returns an `int` or `float`, such as one that calculates and returns the square of a number.
- Create an example of a function that returns a `bool`, such as one that checks if a given number is even or odd.
- Illustrate a function that returns multiple values, like a function that takes a list of numbers and returns both the sum and the average of the list.

## CHAPTER 10

Advanced Functions

W E have learned the fundamental knowledge of functions in Python. However, a single function, as a tiny piece of puzzle, cannot make a comprehensive masterpiece. We need many functions, organized in a professional manner, to perform sophisticated tasks. In this chapter, we are going to learn how to organize functions in various ways, including nested, hierarchical, and recursive structures, to fully explore the creative potential functions hold.

Are you ready? Let's get started!

10.1 NESTED FUNCTIONS

10.1.1 Explanation

Nested function calls occur when the output of one function is immediately used as the input to another function. This allows for streamlined and compact code, especially when performing a sequence of operations. Nested function calls reduce the need for intermediate variables by directly passing outputs to other functions. It also helps in writing more concise and readable code, especially for operations that are logically sequential. At last, it simplifies operations by chaining them together in a single line, making the code easier to follow.

10.1.2 Demonstration

```
print(input('Enter your name: '))
```

```
Enter your name: Neo
Neo
```

Here, the input function prompts the user for their name and returns it. The returned name is immediately passed to the print function, which displays it on the screen. This is a simple example of how nested function calls can reduce the need for extra variables.

DOI: 10.1201/9781003527725-10

```
result = abs(round(-4.567))
print(result)  # Output: 5
```

5

Here, the `round` function rounds the number −4.567 to −5. The `abs` function then takes the output of `round` and returns its absolute value. The nested call simplifies the process into a single line, making the code cleaner.

```
msg = '   hello, World!  '
cleaned_msg = msg.strip().capitalize().replace('world', 'there')
print(cleaned_msg)  # Output: 'Hello, there!'
```

Hello, there!

Here, the `strip()` function removes leading and trailing whitespace, `capitalize` then capitalizes the first letter of the cleaned string, and `replace` substitutes "world" with "there" Each method operates on the output of the previous one, demonstrating how nested function calls can simplify string manipulation.

```
print(len(str(12345)))  # Output: 5
```

5

Here, `str` converts the number 12345 to a string, `len` then calculates the length of the string. This is a basic yet powerful example of how built-in functions can be nested to perform multiple operations in one go.

10.1.3 Practice

Task: Calculator.

1. Define a function `get_number()` that asks the user to input a number
2. Define a function `sum(x, y)` that computes the sum of two numbers x and y
3. Define a function `subtraction(x, y)` that computes the subtraction of two numbers x and y
4. Define a function `product(x, y)` that computes the product of two numbers x and y
5. Define a function `divide(x, y)` that computes the division of two numbers x and y
6. Define a function `arithmetic()` that prints the arithmetic operation result of two numbers by calling functions defined above

```
def get_number():
    n = float(input('Please enter a number: '))
    return n

def sum(x, y):
    return x + y

def substract(x, y):
    return x - y
```

```
def product(x, y):
  return x * y

def divide(x, y):
  return x / y

def arithmetic():
  x = get_number()
  y = get_number()
  print(f'x + y = {sum(x, y)}')
  print(f'x - y = {substract(x, y)}')
  print(f'x * y = {product(x, y)}')
  print(f'x / y = {divide(x, y)}')

arithmetic()
```

```
Please enter a number: 2
Please enter a number: 3
2.0 + 3.0 = 5.0
2.0 - 3.0 = -1.0
2.0 * 3.0 = 6.0
2.0 / 3.0 = 0.6666666666666666
```

Task: Statistics.

1. Define a function `get_number()` that asks the user to input a number
2. Define a function `min(x, y, z)` that computes the min of three numbers x, y, and z
3. Define a function `max(x, y, z)` that computes the max of three numbers x, y, and z
4. Define a function `total(x, y, z)` that computes the total of three numbers x, y, and z
5. Define a function `avg(x, y, z)` that computes the average of three numbers x, y, and z
6. Define a function `stats(x, y, z)` that prints the statistics of the three numbers by calling functions defined above

```
def get_number():
  n = float(input('Please enter a number: '))
  return n

def min(x, y, z):
  min = x
  if y < min:
    min = y
  if z < min:
    min = z
  return min

def max(x, y, z):
  max = x
  if y > max:
    max = y
```

```
    if z > max:
      max = z
    return max

def total(x, y, z):
  return x + y + z

def avg(x, y, z):
  return total(x, y, z) / 3

def stats():
  x = get_number()
  y = get_number()
  z = get_number()
  print(x, y, z,
        'min:', min(x, y, z),
        'max:', max(x, y, z),
        'total:', total(x, y, z),
        'average:', avg(x, y, z))

stats()
```

```
Please enter a number: 1
Please enter a number: 2
Please enter a number: 3
1.0 2.0 3.0 min: 1.0 max: 3.0 total: 6.0 average: 2.0
```

10.2   HIERARCHICAL FUNCTIONS

10.2.1   Explanation

In programming, hierarchical functions refer to breaking down a large task into smaller, more manageable sub-tasks, each of which is handled by a separate function. This approach is often used to improve code readability, maintainability, and modularity. By dividing a complex task into a hierarchy of functions, each function can focus on a specific part of the problem, making the overall logic clearer and easier to manage.

10.2.2   Demonstration

The following program will ask the user to enter the student's name and the grades for three exams. It will then calculate the average grade, assign a letter grade, display the result, and allow for multiple students to be processed in a loop.

```
# Define a function to calculate the average of three grades
def calculate_average(grade1, grade2, grade3):
  total = grade1 + grade2 + grade3
  return total / 3

# Define a function to assign a letter grade based on the average
def assign_letter_grade(average):
  if average >= 90:
    return 'A'
  elif average >= 80:
```

```python
      return 'B'
  elif average >= 70:
      return 'C'
  elif average >= 60:
      return 'D'
  else:
      return 'F'

# Define a function to print the results for a single student
def print_results(name, average, grade):
  print(f'Student: {name}, Average: {average:.2f}, Grade: {grade}')

# Define a function to process a single student's grades
def process_single_student():
  # Ask the user to enter the student's name and grades
  name = input('Enter the student\'s name: ')
  grade1 = float(input('Enter the grade for exam 1: '))
  grade2 = float(input('Enter the grade for exam 2: '))
  grade3 = float(input('Enter the grade for exam 3: '))

  # Calculate the average grade
  average = calculate_average(grade1, grade2, grade3)

  # Assign a letter grade based on the average
  letter_grade = assign_letter_grade(average)

  # Print the result
  print_results(name, average, letter_grade)

# Define a function to process multiple students' grades
def process_student_grades():
  while True:
    process_single_student()

    # Ask if the user wants to process another student
    another = input('Enter another student? (yes/no): ')
    if another != 'yes':
      break

# Run the program
process_student_grades()
```

```
Enter the student's name: Alice
Enter the grade for exam 1: 95
Enter the grade for exam 2: 99
Enter the grade for exam 3: 100
Student:Alice, Average:98.00, Grade:A
Enter another student? (yes/no): yes
Enter the student's name: Bob
Enter the grade for exam 1: 80
Enter the grade for exam 2: 90
Enter the grade for exam 3: 100
Student:Bob, Average:90.00, Grade:A
Enter another student? (yes/no): no
```

In this example, the `calculate_average(grade1, grade2, grade3)` function takes three grades as input, calculates their total, and returns the average. The `assign_letter_grade(average)` function takes the average grade as input and returns a corresponding letter grade (A, B, C, D, or F). The `print_results(name, average, grade)` function prints the student's name, average grade, and final letter grade. The `process_single_student()` function prompts the user to enter the student's name and the grades for three exams. It then calculates the average, assigns a letter grade, and prints the result. The main function `process_student_grades()` runs in a loop, calling `process_single_student()` to process each student. After processing one student, it asks the user if they want to enter another student's grades. If the user enters anything other than `'yes'`, the loop exits and the program ends.

10.3 INTERACT WITH GENAI

Here are some questions and prompts you can interact with generative AI tools, including ChatGPT.

- Explain how to define a function that uses the returned value from another function. Why is this approach useful in programming?
- Discuss how chaining functions together by using the return value of one function as the input for another can make your code more modular and maintainable.
- Describe scenarios where utilizing the return value from another function can simplify complex tasks, such as performing multiple calculations or processing data in stages.
- Illustrate a scenario where a function returns a Boolean value (e.g., checking if a number is prime), and another function uses this value to determine whether to add the number to a list of primes.
- Reflect on how using return values from other functions has impacted your coding process. How does this approach improve code organization and reduce redundancy? Have a conversation with GenAI.
- Submit a Python code snippet where you define and use a function that relies on the returned value from another function to AI and ask "Give me personalized feedback on the structure and efficiency of your functions."
- Describe a challenge you faced when working with functions that depend on the return values of other functions to AI and ask "Explain how to resolve the issue and improve the interaction between my functions."

10.4 RECURSIVE FUNCTIONS

10.4.1 Explanation

Recursion is a programming technique where a function calls itself to solve a problem. The function breaks down the problem into smaller, more manageable subproblems, each of which is solved by the function itself. Recursion can simplify the code for problems that naturally fit a recursive pattern, like tree traversals, sorting algorithms, or mathematical sequences. A recursive function should have two cases: The base case is the condition under which the recursion stops and prevents infinite recursion; the recursive case is the part of the function where the recursion occurs, usually involving the function calling itself with a smaller or simpler input.

10.4.2 Demonstration

Direct recursion refers to a function that directly calls itself within its definition.

```python
def factorial(n):
    if n == 0 or n == 1:
        return 1
    else:
        return n * factorial(n - 1)

print(factorial(5))   # Output: 120
```

120

Indirect recursion refers to a function that is called indirectly through another function, creating a cycle of function calls.

```python
def function_a(n):
    if n > 0:
        return function_b(n - 1)

def function_b(n):
    if n > 0:
        return function_a(n - 2)

print(function_a(5))   # Output: None
```

None

10.4.3 Practice

Task: Define a recursive function `fib(n)` to compute Fibonacci series that follows $fib(0) = 0$, $fib(1) = 1$, $fib(n) = fib(n-1) + fib(n-2)$.

```python
def fib(n):
    if n == 0 or n == 1:
        return n
    else:
        return fib(n - 1) + fib(n - 2)

fib(4)
```

3

Task: Define a recursive function `digits(n)` to compute the number of digits of a positive integer n.

```
def digits(n):
  if n < 10:
    return 1
  else:
    return 1 + digits(n//10)

digits(2022)
```

4

Task: Write a recursive function `is_palindrome(s)` that checks whether a given string `s` is a palindrome (reads the same forward and backward).

For example:

- `''`, `'a'`, `'ada'`, `'adda'` are palindrome;
- `'ab'`, `'abs'` are not palindrome.

We can assume the input string contains only A to Z and a to z, no other special characters, it might be empty, and an empty string is palindrome.

```
def palindrome(s):
  # Base case: if the string is empty or a single character
  # it's a palindrome
  if len(s) <= 1:
    return True
  # Recursive case: check if the first and last characters are the same
  # and recurse on the substring
  else:
    if s[0] == s[-1]:
      return palindrome(s[1:-1])
    else:
      return False

print(palindrome('ada'))
print(palindrome('adba'))
print(palindrome('adccda'))
```

```
True
False
True
```

Task: Write a recursive function `count_ways(n)` that returns the number of ways to climb a staircase with `n` steps if you can take either 1 step or 2 steps at a time.

```
def count_ways(n):
  # Base case: 0 or 1 step has 1 way to climb
  if n == 0 or n == 1:
    return 1
  # Recursive case: sum the ways to climb n-1 steps and n-2 steps
  else:
    return count_ways(n - 1) + count_ways(n - 2)

# Test the function
print(count_ways(4))   # Output: 5
```

5

10.5   INTERACT WITH GENAI

Here are some questions and prompts you can interact with generative AI tools, including ChatGPT.

- Explain what a recursive function is in Python. How does it differ from an iterative function?
- Discuss the concept of base cases and recursive cases in a recursive function. Why is the base case crucial for preventing infinite recursion?
- Describe some common scenarios where recursion is a more suitable approach than iteration. Why might you choose to use recursion?
- Generate an example of a simple recursive function that calculates the factorial of a number. Explain how the function works step by step.
- Provide an example of a recursive function that computes the nth Fibonacci number. Highlight how the function calls itself with different arguments.
- Illustrate a recursive function that reverses a string. Demonstrate how the function breaks the problem down into smaller subproblems.
- Submit a Python code snippet where you define and use a recursive function to AI and ask "give me personalized feedback on the correctness, efficiency, and clarity of my recursion."
- Describe a challenge you faced when working with recursion, such as reaching the maximum recursion depth or getting stuck in an infinite loop to AI and ask. "suggest ways to fix or optimize my recursive function."

III

Data Structures

S ECTION III: DATA STRUCTURES introduces the concept and importance of data structures in Python, which are crucial for efficiently storing and organizing data. You will explore Python's built-in data structures: lists, tuples, sets, and dictionaries. The section covers how to create each of these structures, access their elements, and perform various manipulations using Python's built-in methods. Understanding these data structures will enable you to handle and process data more effectively in your programs.

The learning objectives for this section are as follows:

- Understand the role and significance of data structures in programming.

- Create and work with lists to store and manipulate ordered collections of items.

- Use tuples to handle immutable sequences of data.

- Implement sets to manage unordered collections of unique elements.

- Utilize dictionaries for storing key-value pairs and accessing data efficiently.

## CHAPTER 11

List

D ATA STRUCTURES are essential for organizing and managing data effectively in programming, and Python's list is one of the most widely used structures. A list allows you to store an ordered collection of items, which can be of any type, and provides powerful tools for accessing, modifying, and iterating through data. In this chapter, we are going to learn what a list is, how to create, access, slice, and manipulate a list, and the Pythonic way of creating a list using list comprehension. Are you excited? Let's get started!

11.1 WHAT IS A LIST

In Python, a list is a versatile and dynamic data structure that allows for the storage and manipulation of collections of elements. Unlike arrays in some other programming languages, Python lists can hold elements of different data types and can be easily modified and resized. Lists are ordered collections, meaning that the order in which elements are added is preserved, and elements can be accessed and manipulated based on their position within the list.

One of the primary advantages of Python lists is their convenience and flexibility. Lists provide a straightforward and intuitive way to organize and work with data, making them suitable for a wide range of applications. Additionally, Python lists offer efficient random access to elements, allowing for quick retrieval and modification of individual items based on their index. This efficiency makes lists well-suited for tasks that involve accessing and modifying elements at arbitrary positions within the collection.

Common use cases for Python lists include storing and processing sequential data, such as lists of numbers, strings, or objects. Lists are often used in algorithms that require dynamic resizing or rearranging of data, such as sorting, searching, or filtering operations. They are also frequently employed in data processing tasks, where the ability to iterate over and manipulate collections of data is essential. Overall, Python lists serve as versatile and indispensable tools for managing and manipulating data in a wide variety of programming scenarios.

11.2 CREATE A LIST

11.2.1 Demonstration

In Python, there are several methods for creating lists, providing flexibility and convenience for different programming scenarios. One common method is to use the list constructor, which initializes an empty list or converts another iterable object, such as a tuple or string, into a list.

```python
my_list_1 = list() # Create an empty list
print(my_list_1)
```

```
[]
```

```python
my_list_2 = list('Hello, world') # Create a list from a string
print(my_list_2)
```

```
['H', 'e', 'l', 'l', 'o', ',', ' ', 'w', 'o', 'r', 'l', 'd']
```

Another approach to creating lists in Python is by direct assignment, where we manually specify the elements of the list within square brackets.

```python
my_list_3 = [1, 3, 2, 4, 6] # Create a list of integers
print(my_list_3)
```

```
[1, 3, 2, 4, 6]
```

```python
my_list_4 = ['Hello', 'world'] # Create a list of Strings
print(my_list_4)
```

```
['Hello', 'world']
```

```python
my_list_5 = [1.5, 1.6, 1.8, 2.0] # Create a list of floats
print(my_list_5)
```

```
[1.5, 1.6, 1.8, 2.0]
```

In Python, the built-in function `len()` is used to determine the length or the number of elements in a list. When applied to a list, `len()` returns an integer representing the total count of elements contained within the list. This count includes all individual elements, regardless of their data type or complexity, providing a convenient way to quickly assess the length of the list.

```python
print(my_list_1)
print(len(my_list_1)) # output 0
```

```
[]
0
```

```python
print(my_list_2)
print(len(my_list_2)) # output 12
```

```
['H', 'e', 'l', 'l', 'o', ',', ' ', 'w', 'o', 'r', 'l', 'd']
12
```

```
print(my_list_3)
print(len(my_list_3)) # output 5
```

```
[1, 3, 2, 4, 6]
5
```

```
print(my_list_4)
print(len(my_list_4)) # output 2
```

```
['Hello', 'world']
2
```

```
print(my_list_5)
print(len(my_list_5)) # output 4
```

```
[1.5, 1.6, 1.8, 2.0]
4
```

11.2.2 Practice

Task: Create a list, list1, from a string 'List Constructor'. Print the list together with its length.

```
list1 = list('List Constructor')
print(list1, len(list1))
```

```
['L', 'i', 's', 't', ' ', 'C', 'o', 'n', 's', 't', 'r', 'u', 'c', 't', 'o', 'r'] 16
```

Task: Create a list, list2, containing some integers. Print the list together with its length.

```
list2 = [2, 5, 3, 4, 1]
print(list2, len(list2))
```

```
[2, 5, 3, 4, 1] 5
```

Task: Create a list, list3, containing some floats. Print the list together with its length.

```
list3 = [2.1, 5.2, 3.3, 4.4, 1.5]
print(list2, len(list3))
```

```
[2, 5, 3, 4, 1] 5
```

Task: Create a list, list4 containing strings. Print the list together with its length.

```
list4 = ['2', '5', '3', '4', '1']
print(list4, len(list4))
```

```
['2', '5', '3', '4', '1'] 5
```

11.3 HETEROGENEITY

11.3.1 Demonstration

Python lists are incredibly flexible data structures that can contain elements of different data types within the same list. This flexibility stems from Python's dynamic typing system, which allows variables to hold values of any data type without requiring explicit declaration. As a result, lists in Python can seamlessly accommodate a mix of integers, floats, strings, Booleans, and even other lists or complex objects.

This capability is particularly advantageous in scenarios where heterogeneous data needs to be stored and manipulated together. For example, a list representing a student record might include elements such as the student's name (a string), age (an integer), Grade Point Average (a float), and whether they are enrolled in a particular course (a Boolean). By storing these diverse data types within a single list, Python simplifies data management and reduces the need for separate data structures or complex data models.

Furthermore, the ability for Python lists to contain different types of values fosters code simplicity and readability. Developers can organize related data elements into a single list, making it easier to access and manipulate them as a cohesive unit. This flexibility aligns with Python's philosophy of readability and ease of use, allowing programmers to express their intentions clearly and concisely without sacrificing functionality.

```
my_list_6 = [1, 'Hello', 1.5, [1.5, 1.6, 1.8, 2.0], my_list_4]
print(my_list_6)
```

```
[1, 'Hello', 1.5, [1.5, 1.6, 1.8, 2.0], ['Hello', 'world']]
```

```
student = ['David Wood', 18, 3.9, True]
print(student)
```

```
['David Wood', 18, 3.9, True]
```

Note that len() counts the number of elements in a list. If the element is another list, it is still counted as one. The list [1.5, 1.6, 1.8, 2.0] in my_list_6 counts one, and the list ['Hello', 'world'] in my_list_6 counts one, too.

```
print(my_list_6)
print(len(my_list_6)) # output 5
```

```
[1, 'Hello', 1.5, [1.5, 1.6, 1.8, 2.0], ['Hello', 'world']]
5
```

```
print(student)
print(len(student)) # output 4
```

```
['David Wood', 18, 3.9, True]
4
```

11.3.2 Practice

Task: Create a list `list5` contains some numbers (combination of int and float). Print the list together with its length.

```
list5 = [2.1, 5.2, 3, 4, 1]
print(list5, len(list5))
```

[2.1, 5.2, 3, 4, 1] 5

Task: Create a list `list6` contains all the list you created above. Print the list together with its length.

```
list6 = [list1, list2, list3, list4, list5]
print(list6, len(list6))
```

[['L', 'i', 's', 't', ' ', 'C', 'o', 'n', 's', 't', 'r', 'u', 'c', 't', 'o', 'r'],
[2, 5, 3, 4, 1], [2.1, 5.2, 3.3, 4.4, 1.5], ['2', '5', '3', '4', '1'],
[2.1, 5.2, 3, 4, 1]] 5

Task: Create a list, `list7`, containing following values:

1. Customer name (`str`)
2. Product name (`str`)
3. Product price (`float`)
4. Product quantity (`int`)
5. Paid_status (`bool`).

Print the list together with its length.

```
list7 = ['Neo', 'iPhone', 999.99, 2, True]
print(list7, len(list7))
```

['Neo', 'iPhone', 999.99, 2, True] 5

11.3.3 Test your understanding

Task: Why Python's list can contain multiple data types? Explain it to yourself (ideally, someone else).

Answer: Python's dynamic typing system facilitates the creation of heterogeneous lists by associating variables with references to objects rather than directly with the objects themselves. In a Python list, elements are actually references (or addresses) pointing to the memory locations where the objects are stored. While the references stored in the list can be of different data types, they ultimately point to objects that can vary in data type as well. This mechanism allows Python lists to seamlessly accommodate a mix of integers, floats, strings, Booleans, and other data types within the same list. Thus, the heterogeneity of Python lists arises from the flexibility of Python's dynamic typing system, which enables references in the list to point to objects of different data types while maintaining consistency in how these references are stored and accessed.

11.4   ACCESS A LIST BY INDEX

11.4.1   Demonstration

In Python, accessing elements in a list is done using indices, which represent the positions of the elements within the list. Similar to other programming languages like Java and C++, Python starts indexing from 0, meaning that the first element of the list is at index 0, the second element is at index 1, and so on. This indexing convention may differ from other languages like R, which starts indexing from 1. It's important to note that the index of the last element in a list is always one less than the length of the list. For example, if a list has five elements, the last element is at index `len(list)` -1. Attempting to access an index larger than `len(list)` -1 will result in an error, as it exceeds the bounds of the list.

```python
# Define a list of fruits

my_list = ['apple', 'banana', 'orange']
```

```python
# Accessing the first element of the list
print(my_list[0])  # Output: 'apple'
```

```
apple
```

```python
# Accessing the third element of the list
print(my_list[2])  # Output: 'orange'
```

```
orange
```

```python
# Accessing the last element of the list
print(my_list[len(my_list) - 1])  # Output: 'orange'
```

```
orange
```

```python
# Attempting to access an index larger than len(list) - 1
# This will result in an IndexError
print(my_list[3])  # IndexError: list index out of range
```

```
---------------------------------------------------------------------
IndexError                              Traceback (most recent call last)
<ipython-input-4-ccaedad31e7a> in <cell line: 3>()
      1 # Attempting to access an index larger than len(list) - 1
      2 # This will result in an IndexError
----> 3 print(my_list[3])  # IndexError: list index out of range

IndexError: list index out of range
```

Using the `len()` function, we can easily determine the index of the last element in the list. By subtracting 1 from the length of the list, we obtain the index of the last element, allowing us to access it directly using -1. Similarly, we can use -2 to access the second-to-last element, -3 for the third-to-last element, and so forth. Note that the first element has index of `-len()` and if we use an index less than it, we will get an error.

This negative indexing scheme simplifies the process of accessing elements from the end of the list and enhances the readability of Python code when dealing with list manipulation or traversal from right to left. This feature is particularly useful when working with lists of unknown or variable length, as it provides a convenient way to access elements relative to the end of the list without needing to calculate the exact index.

```python
# Define a list of fruits
fruits = ['apple', 'banana', 'orange', 'grape', 'kiwi']
```

```python
# Accessing the last element of the list using negative index
print(fruits[-1])   # Output: 'kiwi'
```

kiwi

```python
# Accessing the second-to-last element of the list using negative index
print(fruits[-2])   # Output: 'grape'
```

grape

```python
# Accessing the third-to-last element of the list using negative index
print(fruits[-3])   # Output: 'orange'
```

orange

```python
# Accessing the first element of the list using negative index
print(fruits[-len(fruits)])   # Output: 'apple'
```

apple

```python
# Attempting to access an index beyond the range of negative indices
# This will result in an IndexError
print(fruits[-6])   # IndexError: list index out of range
```

```
---------------------------------------------------------------------
IndexError                              Traceback (most recent call last)
<ipython-input-28-d712c38661af> in <cell line: 3>()
      1 # Attempting to access an index beyond the range of negative indices
      2 # This will result in an IndexError
----> 3 print(fruits[-6])   # IndexError: list index out of range

IndexError: list index out of range
```

11.4.2   Practice

```python
# Run this cell for these practice
list_practice = [1, 3, 5, 7, 9]
```

Task: Print the first element in `list_practice` using non-negative index

```python
list_practice[0]
```

1

Task: Print the 2nd element in `list_practice` using non-negative index

```
list_practice[1]
```

3

Task: Print the 3rd element in `list_practice` using non-negative index

```
list_practice[2]
```

5

Task: Print the last element in `list_practice` using non-negative index

```
list_practice[len(list_practice) - 1]
```

9

Task: Print the last element in `list_practice` using negative index

```
list_practice[-1]
```

9

Task: Print the first element in `list_practice` using negative index

```
list_practice[-len(list_practice)]
```

1

Task: Find a positive index that will result in an error

```
list_practice[6]
```

```
---------------------------------------------------------------------
IndexError                                Traceback (most recent call last)
<ipython-input-15-d410d82fc72c> in <cell line: 1>()
----> 1 list_practice[6]

IndexError: list index out of range
```

Task: Find a negative index that will result in an error

```
list_practice[-6]
```

```
---------------------------------------------------------------------
IndexError                                Traceback (most recent call last)
<ipython-input-16-7946a41bc3f5> in <cell line: 1>()
----> 1 list_practice[-6]

IndexError: list index out of range
```

11.5 ACCESS A LIST BY ITERATION

11.5.1 Demonstration

Iterating through a Python list allows for the sequential processing of each element within the list. One common method of iteration involves using indices to access elements individually, where a loop iterates over the indices of the list and accesses each element using its corresponding index. While this approach provides direct access to individual elements, it requires explicit index management and can be more verbose compared to directly iterating over the elements of the list. On the other hand, iterating directly over the elements of the list eliminates the need for index manipulation, resulting in cleaner and more concise code.

Using a for loop to iterate directly over the elements of a list simplifies the iteration process by abstracting away the index management. This approach is often preferred in Python for its readability and simplicity. By iterating directly over the elements, the loop automatically accesses each element in sequence, without the need to track or manage indices manually. This leads to more concise and expressive code, enhancing code readability and reducing the likelihood of errors due to index mismanagement.

```python
# Define a list of numbers
numbers = [1, 2, 3, 4, 5]

# Iterate using index-based iteration
for i in range(len(numbers)):
    print(numbers[i])   # Accessing elements using index

# Iterate using direct iteration
for num in numbers:
    print(num)   # Accessing elements directly
```

```
1
2
3
4
5
1
2
3
4
5
```

In these examples, we iterate through the list numbers using both index-based iteration and direct iteration approaches. In the index-based iteration, we use a for loop to iterate over the indices of the list and access each element using its corresponding index. In contrast, the direct iteration approach simplifies the process by directly iterating over the elements of the list, eliminating the need for index manipulation. This results in cleaner and more concise code, enhancing readability and reducing potential errors.

11.5.2 Practice

```python
# Run this cell for this practice
numbers = [1, 2, 2, 2, 3, 4, 4, 5]
```

Task: Print each element in **numbers** on a new line using a for loop for iteration.

```python
for i in numbers:
  print(i)
```

```
1
2
2
2
3
4
4
5
```

Task: Calculate the sum in **numbers** using a for loop for iteration and print the sum.

```python
total = 0
for i in numbers:
  total += i
print(total)
```

23

Task: Count how many 4 in **numbers** using a for loop for iteration and print the count.

```python
count_4 = 0
for i in numbers:
  if i == 4:
    count_4 +=1
print(count_4)
```

2

Task: Count the number of even integers in **numbers** using a for loop for iteration and print the count.

```python
count_even = 0
for i in numbers:
  if i %2 == 0:
    count_even +=1
print(count_even)
```

5

11.6 LIST MANIPULATION

11.6.1 Demonstration

Python lists offer a variety of built-in functions for efficient manipulation and management of list elements. One of the most commonly used functions is **append()**, which adds a new element to the end of the list, expanding its size by one. This function is useful for dynamically growing lists as new elements are generated or retrieved during program execution. Conversely, the **remove()** function allows for the removal of a specific element from the list based on its value, effectively reducing the size of the list by one. Additionally, the **insert()** function enables the insertion of a new element at a specified position within the list, allowing for targeted modification of list contents.

These functions provide essential tools for adding, removing, and inserting elements into Python lists, facilitating dynamic data management in various programming scenarios.

```
# Create a list of numbers
my_list = [1, 2, 3, 4, 5]
```

```
# Append a new element to the list
my_list.append(6)
print(my_list)  # Output: [1, 2, 3, 4, 5, 6]
```

```
[1, 2, 3, 4, 5, 6]
```

```
# Remove the element with value 3 from the list
my_list.remove(3)
print(my_list)  # Output: [1, 2, 4, 5, 6]
```

```
[1, 2, 4, 5, 6]
```

```
# Insert the value 10 at index 2
my_list.insert(2, 10)
print(my_list)  # Output: [1, 2, 10, 4, 5, 6]
```

```
[1, 2, 10, 4, 5, 6]
```

11.6.2 Practice

```
# Define a list of fruits and run it for this practice
fruits = ['apple', 'banana', 'orange', 'grape', 'kiwi']
```

Task: Add a new fruit, `'pear'`, to the end of the list `fruits` using the `append()` function.

```
fruits.append('pear')
fruits
```

```
['apple', 'banana', 'orange', 'grape', 'kiwi', 'pear']
```

Task: Remove the fruit `'banana'` from the list `fruits` using the `remove()` function.

```
fruits.remove('banana')
fruits
```

```
['apple', 'orange', 'grape', 'kiwi', 'pear']
```

Task: Insert the fruit `'blueberry'` at index 2 in the list `fruits` using the `insert()` function.

```
fruits.insert(2, 'blueberry')
fruits
```

```
['apple', 'orange', 'blueberry', 'grape', 'kiwi', 'pear']
```

11.7   MORE MANIPULATION OF A LIST

11.7.1   Demonstration

In addition to the basic list manipulation functions, Python lists offer several other useful functions for more advanced operations. The `extend()` function is used to append elements from another iterable (such as another list) to the end of the current list, effectively extending its length. This function is particularly handy when combining multiple lists into one. The `reverse()` function reverses the order of elements in the list, providing a convenient way to rearrange list contents. Finally, the `sort()` function sorts the elements of the list in ascending order by default, allowing for easy sorting of list elements. These functions provide additional flexibility and functionality for working with Python lists, enabling more sophisticated list manipulation operations.

```python
# Define a list of integers
my_list = [1, 2, 3, 4, 5]
```

```python
# Extend the list with another list
additional_list = [5, 6]
my_list.extend(additional_list)
print(my_list)
```

```
[1, 2, 3, 4, 5, 5, 6]
```

```python
# Reverse the order of elements in the list
my_list.reverse()
print(my_list)
```

```
[6, 5, 5, 4, 3, 2, 1]
```

```python
# Sort the elements of the list ascendingly
my_list.sort()
print(my_list)
```

```
[1, 2, 3, 4, 5, 5, 6]
```

```python
# Sort the elements of the list descendingly
my_list.sort(reverse = True)
print(my_list)
```

```
[6, 5, 5, 4, 3, 2, 1]
```

Furthermore, Python lists offer functions such as `clear()` for removing all elements from the list, effectively resetting it to an empty state. The `del` statement, while not a function, serves a similar purpose by allowing for the deletion of list elements or slices based on their indices. These functions and statements provide flexibility in list manipulation, allowing developers to tailor list contents to meet specific requirements during program execution.

```python
# Delete the element at index 2
my_list = [1, 2, 3, 4, 5]
del my_list[2]
print(my_list)   # Output: [1, 2, 4, 5]
```

```
[1, 2, 4, 5]
```

```
# Clear all elements from the list
my_list.clear()
print(my_list)   # Output: []
```

```
[]
```

In addition to the list manipulation functions provided by Python, there are other techniques for combining and sorting lists. Concatenating two lists involves combining their elements to form a single list. This can be achieved using the + operator, which concatenates the elements of one list with the elements of another. This method is straightforward and effective for combining lists when the order of elements is preserved.

Additionally, the `sorted()` function offers a versatile way to sort the elements of a list. Unlike the `sort()` method, which sorts the list in place, the `sorted()` function returns a new list containing the sorted elements, leaving the original list unchanged. This provides a non-destructive way to obtain a sorted version of a list, making it useful for scenarios where preserving the original list is important.

```
# Concatenate two lists
list1 = [1, 2, 3]
list2 = [4, 5, 6]
concatenated_list = list1 + list2
print(concatenated_list)   # Output: [1, 2, 3, 4, 5, 6]
```

```
[1, 2, 3, 4, 5, 6]
```

```
# Sorted function
unsorted_list = [3, 1, 4, 2, 5]
sorted_list = sorted(unsorted_list)
print(sorted_list)   # Output: [1, 2, 3, 4, 5]
print(unsorted_list)   # Output: [3, 1, 4, 2, 5]
```

```
[1, 2, 3, 4, 5]
[3, 1, 4, 2, 5]
```

11.7.2 Practice

Task: Extend the list `fruits` with a new list `['pineapple', 'strawberry']` using the `extend()` function.

```
fruits.extend(['pineapple', 'strawberry'])
fruits
```

```
['apple',
 'orange',
 'blueberry',
 'grape',
 'kiwi',
 'pear',
 'pineapple',
 'strawberry']
```

Task: Reverse the order of elements in the list `fruits` using the `reverse()` function.

```
fruits.reverse()
fruits
```

```
['strawberry',
 'pineapple',
 'pear',
 'kiwi',
 'grape',
 'blueberry',
 'orange',
 'apple']
```

Task: Sort the elements in the list `fruits` in alphabetical order using the `sort()` function.

```
fruits.sort()
fruits
```

```
['apple',
 'blueberry',
 'grape',
 'kiwi',
 'orange',
 'pear',
 'pineapple',
 'strawberry']
```

Task: Delete the fruit at index 1 from the list `fruits` using the `del` statement.

```
del fruits[1]
fruits
```

```
['apple', 'grape', 'kiwi', 'orange', 'pear', 'pineapple', 'strawberry']
```

Task: Concatenate the `fruits` list with itself and store the result in a new list called `doubled_fruits`. Print the doubled list.

```
double_fruits = fruits + fruits
double_fruits
```

```
['apple',
 'grape',
 'kiwi',
 'orange',
 'pear',
 'pineapple',
 'strawberry',
 'apple',
 'grape',
 'kiwi',
 'orange',
 'pear',
 'pineapple',
 'strawberry']
```

Task: Create a new list called `more_fruits` containing the fruits `'blackberry'` and `'melon'`, then concatenate it with the existing `fruits` list. Print the concatenated list.

```
more_fruits = ['blackberry', 'melon']
fruits += more_fruits
fruits
```

```
['apple',
 'grape',
 'kiwi',
 'orange',
 'pear',
 'pineapple',
 'strawberry',
 'blackberry',
 'melon']
```

Task: Sort the "fruits" list in alphabetical order using the `sorted()` function. Print both the sorted list and the original list.

```
fruits_ordered = sorted(fruits)
fruits, fruits_ordered
```

```
(['apple',
  'grape',
  'kiwi',
  'orange',
  'pear',
  'pineapple',
  'strawberry',
  'blackberry',
  'melon'],
 ['apple',
  'blackberry',
  'grape',
  'kiwi',
  'melon',
  'orange',
  'pear',
  'pineapple',
  'strawberry'])
```

11.8   SLICE A LIST

11.8.1   Demonstration

Slicing in Python allows for the extraction of a subset of elements from a list using a specified range of indices. When using non-negative indices, slicing involves specifying the starting index, ending index (exclusive), and an optional step size. The syntax for slicing is `list[start:end:step]`, where `start` indicates the index of the first element to include, `end` indicates the index after the last element to include, and `step` determines the increment between consecutive indices. If any of these parameters are omitted, default values are used: `start` defaults to 0, `end` defaults to the length of the list, and `step` defaults to 1. Slicing with non-negative indices provides a flexible way to extract contiguous portions of a list, allowing for efficient data manipulation and analysis.

```python
# Define a list of numbers
numbers = [0, 1, 2, 3, 4, 5, 6, 7, 8, 9]
```

```python
# Slicing with non-negative indices
print(numbers[2:7])      # Output: [2, 3, 4, 5, 6]
```

```
[2, 3, 4, 5, 6]
```

```python
print(numbers[:5])       # Output: [0, 1, 2, 3, 4]
```

```
[0, 1, 2, 3, 4]
```

```python
print(numbers[3:])       # Output: [3, 4, 5, 6, 7, 8, 9]
```

```
[3, 4, 5, 6, 7, 8, 9]
```

```python
print(numbers[::2])      # Output: [0, 2, 4, 6, 8]
```

```
[0, 2, 4, 6, 8]
```

```python
print(numbers[1:8:3])    # Output: [1, 4, 7]
```

```
[1, 4, 7]
```

On the other hand, slicing with negative indices involves specifying indices relative to the end of the list. Negative indices count backward from the last element of the list, with -1 representing the last element, -2 representing the second-to-last element, and so on. When using negative indices for slicing, the same syntax (`list[start:end:step]`) applies, with negative indices indicating positions from the end of the list. Slicing with negative indices enables the extraction of elements from the end of the list, providing convenient access to elements in reverse order or other non-traditional patterns.

```python
# Slicing with negative indices
print(numbers[-5:])      # Output: [5, 6, 7, 8, 9]
```

```
[5, 6, 7, 8, 9]
```

```python
print(numbers[:-3])      # Output: [0, 1, 2, 3, 4, 5, 6]
```

```
[0, 1, 2, 3, 4, 5, 6]
```

```python
print(numbers[::-1])     # Output: [9, 8, 7, 6, 5, 4, 3, 2, 1, 0]
```

```
[9, 8, 7, 6, 5, 4, 3, 2, 1, 0]
```

Combining both non-negative and negative indices in slicing provides a powerful mechanism for extracting subsets of elements from Python lists with flexibility and precision.

```
# Define a list of letters
letters = ['a', 'b', 'c', 'd', 'e', 'f', 'g', 'h', 'i', 'j']
```

```
# Slicing with a combination of non-negative and negative indices
print(letters[2:-3])      # Output: ['c', 'd', 'e', 'f', 'g']
```

```
['c', 'd', 'e', 'f', 'g']
```

```
print(letters[-5:7])      # Output: ['f', 'g']
```

```
['f', 'g']
```

```
print(letters[4:-2:2])    # Output: ['e', 'g']
```

```
['e', 'g']
```

```
print(letters[-7:3])      # Output: []
```

```
[]
```

```
print(letters[::3])       # Output: ['a', 'd', 'g', 'j']
```

```
['a', 'd', 'g', 'j']
```

```
print(letters[-3::-1])  # Output: ['h', 'g', 'f', 'e', 'd', 'c', 'b', 'a']
```

```
['h', 'g', 'f', 'e', 'd', 'c', 'b', 'a']
```

11.8.2 Practice

```
# Define fruits and run it for this practice
fruits = ['apple', 'banana', 'kiwi', 'orange', 'pineapple']
```

Task: Extract the first three fruits from the list `fruits` using slicing with non-negative indices.

```
fruits[:3]
```

```
['apple', 'banana', 'kiwi']
```

Task: Extract the last two fruits from the list `fruits` using slicing with negative indices.

```
fruits[-2:]
```

```
['orange', 'pineapple']
```

Task: Extract the middle fruits after the first and before the last from the list `fruits` using slicing with a combination of non-negative and negative indices.

```
fruits[1:-1]
```

```
['banana', 'kiwi', 'orange']
```

Task: Extract the sublist that contains every other fruit from the list `fruits`.

```
fruits[::2]
```

```
['apple', 'kiwi', 'pineapple']
```

Task: Extract a sublist from the list `fruits` containing the second, third, and fourth fruits using slicing with non-negative indices.

```
fruits[1:4]
```

```
['banana', 'kiwi', 'orange']
```

Task: Reverse the order of elements in the list `fruits` using slicing with negative indices.

```
fruits[::-1]
```

```
['pineapple', 'orange', 'kiwi', 'banana', 'apple']
```

Task: Extract a sublist from the list `fruits` containing every third fruit, starting from the second fruit.

```
fruits[1::3]
```

```
['banana', 'pineapple']
```

11.9 LIST COMPREHENSION

11.9.1 Demonstration

List comprehension in Python is a concise and elegant way to create lists based on existing lists or other iterables. It allows for the creation of lists in a single line of code, eliminating the need for explicit loop constructs like `for` loops. List comprehension follows a simple syntax that resembles mathematical notation, making it easy to read and understand. The basic structure of list comprehension consists of an expression followed by a `for` clause, which specifies the iteration over elements, optionally followed by additional `for` or `if` clauses for nested iterations or filtering.

The general syntax is:

```
list_variable = [expression for item in iterable condition]
```

```
# Using a for loop to generate a list of squared numbers
squared_numbers = []
for num in range(6):
    squared_numbers.append(num)
print(squared_numbers)                 # Output: [0, 1, 2, 3, 4, 5]


# Using list comprehension for the same task
squared_numbers_comprehension = [num for num in range(6)]
print(squared_numbers_comprehension)# Output: [0, 1, 2, 3, 4, 5]
```

```
[0, 1, 2, 3, 4, 5]
[0, 1, 2, 3, 4, 5]
```

In list comprehension, the optional `if` clause allows for conditional filtering of elements from the original iterable based on a specified condition. This clause enables developers to include or exclude elements from the resulting list based on whether a given condition evaluates to `True` or `False`. The syntax for the `if` clause in list comprehension follows the expression `if condition`, where condition is the Boolean expression that determines whether an element should be included in the resulting list.

```python
# Original list of numbers
numbers = [1, 2, 3, 4, 5, 6, 7, 8, 9, 10]

# Using a for loop to filter even numbers
even_numbers = []
for num in numbers:
  if num % 2 == 0:
    even_numbers.append(num)
print(even_numbers)   # Output: [2, 4, 6, 8, 10]

# List comprehension to filter even numbers
even_numbers_comprehension = [num for num in numbers if num % 2 == 0]

print(even_numbers_comprehension)   # Output: [2, 4, 6, 8, 10]
```

```
[2, 4, 6, 8, 10]
[2, 4, 6, 8, 10]
```

In list comprehension, the final element that we put in the list is the result of an expression or function applied to each element of the original iterable. This allows us to transform or manipulate the elements of the original iterable before they are added to the resulting list. The expression or function specified as the final element can be any valid Python expression or function that operates on the elements of the original iterable.

```python
# Original list of numbers
numbers = [1, 2, 3, 4, 5]

squared_numbers = []
for num in numbers:
  squared_numbers.append(num ** 2)
print(squared_numbers)   # Output: [1, 4, 9, 16, 25]

# List comprehension to square each number
squared_numbers_comprehension = [num ** 2 for num in numbers]

print(squared_numbers_comprehension)   # Output: [1, 4, 9, 16, 25]
```

```
[1, 4, 9, 16, 25]
[1, 4, 9, 16, 25]
```

11.9.2   Practice

```
# Define lists and run this cell for this practice
numbers1 = [1, 2, 3, 4, 5]
numbers2 = [6, 7, 8, 9, 10]
```

Task: Generate a list called `power_of_2` containing the powers of 2 up to the corresponding number in `numbers1`.

```
power_of_2 = [x**2 for x in numbers1]
power_of_2
```

[1, 4, 9, 16, 25]

Task: Create a list called `negative_numbers` containing the negative versions of numbers from `numbers2`.

```
negative_numbers = [-x for x in numbers2]
negative_numbers
```

[-6, -7, -8, -9, -10]

Task: Generate a list called `greater_than_7` containing numbers from `numbers1` that are greater than 7.

```
greater_than_7 = [x for x in numbers1 if x > 7]
greater_than_7
```

[]

Task: Create a list called `even_squares` containing the squares of even numbers from `numbers1`.

```
even_squares = [x**2 for x in numbers1 if x %2 == 0]
even_squares
```

[4, 16]

Task: Generate a list called `divisible_by_3` containing numbers from `numbers2` that are divisible by 3.

```
divisible_by_3 = [x for x in numbers2 if x %3 == 0]
divisible_by_3
```

[6, 9]

Task: Create a list called `odd_multiples_of_3` containing multiples of 3 of odd numbers from `numbers2`.

```
odd_multiples_of_3 = [x*3 for x in numbers2 if x %3 == 0]
odd_multiples_of_3
```

[18, 27]

11.10 ADVANCED LIST COMPREHENSION

11.10.1 Demonstration

Nested iteration in list comprehension allows for the creation of lists with multiple levels of iteration, enabling more complex data manipulation and generation. This advanced technique involves using nested for loops within the list comprehension syntax to iterate over multiple iterables simultaneously. Each nested for loop corresponds to a level of iteration, with the innermost loop iterating over the elements of the innermost iterable. Nested iteration is particularly useful when dealing with nested data structures like lists of lists or lists of tuples, where elements are organized hierarchically.

```python
# Original list of lists (matrix)
matrix = [[1, 2, 3], [4, 5, 6], [7, 8, 9]]

# Flattening the matrix using nested iteration
flattened_matrix = [num for sublist in matrix for num in sublist]

print(flattened_matrix)  # Output: [1, 2, 3, 4, 5, 6, 7, 8, 9]
```

```
[1, 2, 3, 4, 5, 6, 7, 8, 9]
```

Nested iteration can also be extended to find all combinations of elements from multiple lists. This advanced technique involves using multiple nested for loops within the list comprehension syntax, each corresponding to an iterable representing a list. By iterating over each element from each list simultaneously, we can generate all possible combinations of elements across multiple lists. This approach is particularly useful when dealing with scenarios where we need to explore all possible combinations of elements from different sources, such as when generating permutations or combinations of items for various tasks or analyses. Nested iteration allows for a systematic and efficient exploration of all possible combinations, making it a powerful tool for solving a wide range of combinatorial problems in Python programming.

```python
# Two lists of numbers
list1 = [1, 2, 3]
list2 = [3, 4, 5]

# Nested iteration to get all combinations of elements from the two lists
combinations = [(i, j) for i in list1 for j in list2 if i != j]

print(combinations)
```

```
[(1, 3), (1, 4), (1, 5), (2, 3), (2, 4), (2, 5), (3, 4), (3, 5)]
```

```python
# A list of fruits
fruits = ['apple', 'banana', 'orange']

# Nested iteration to get all combinations of fruits from the same list
combinations = [(f1, f2) for f1 in fruits for f2 in fruits if f1 != f2]

print(combinations)
```

```
[('apple', 'banana'), ('apple', 'orange'), ('banana', 'apple'),
('banana', 'orange'), ('orange', 'apple'), ('orange', 'banana')]
```

The `zip()` function in Python is a built-in function that allows for the simultaneous iteration over multiple lists or iterables. It takes multiple iterables as input and returns an iterator that produces tuples containing elements from each of the input iterables. This enables parallel processing of corresponding elements from different iterables, making it convenient for tasks such as combining data from multiple sources or iterating over multiple lists.

```
# Two lists of names and ages
names = ['Alice', 'Bob', 'Charlie']
ages = [25, 30, 35]

# Using zip() in list comprehension to combine elements
combined = [[name, age] for name, age in zip(names, ages)]

print(combined)  # Output: [['Alice', 25], ['Bob', 30], ['Charlie', 35]]
```

```
[['Alice', 25], ['Bob', 30], ['Charlie', 35]]
```

11.10.2 Practice

```
# Define lists and run this cell for this practice
numbers1 = [1, 2, 3, 4, 5]
numbers2 = [6, 7, 8, 9, 10]
```

Task: Create a list called `sum_less_than_10` containing a pair of numbers one from `numbers1` and the other one from `numbers2` and their sum is less than 10.

```
sum_less_than_10 = [[a, b] for a in numbers1 for b in numbers2 if a+b < 10]
sum_less_than_10
```

```
[[1, 6], [1, 7], [1, 8], [2, 6], [2, 7], [3, 6]]
```

Task: Create a list called `sums` containing the sum of corresponding elements from `numbers1` and `numbers2`.

```
sum = [a + b for a, b in zip(numbers1, numbers2)]
sum
```

```
[7, 9, 11, 13, 15]
```

Task: Generate a list called `products` containing the product of corresponding elements from `numbers1` and `numbers2`.

```
products = [a * b for a, b in zip(numbers1, numbers2)]
products
```

```
[6, 14, 24, 36, 50]
```

Task: Create a list called `differences` containing the absolute differences of corresponding elements from `numbers1` and `numbers2`.

```
def abs(x):
  if x < 0:
    return -x

differences = [abs(a - b) for a, b in zip(numbers1, numbers2)]
differences
```

[5, 5, 5, 5, 5]

Here, let's summarize what we learned about list in Table 11.1.

Table 11.1 Summary of Python lists.

Feature	Syntax	Examples
Creation	[] or list()	my_list = [1, 2, 3] my_list = list((1, 2, 3))
Accessing	list[index]	my_list[0] returns 1 my_list[-1] returns 3
Slicing	list[start:stop:step]	my_list = [1, 2, 3] my_list[1:3] returns [2, 3] my_list[::2] returns [1, 3]
Appending	list.append(item)	my_list = [1, 2, 3] my_list.append(4) my_list ⇒ [1, 2, 3, 4]
Extending	list.extend(iterable)	my_list = [1, 2, 3] my_list.extend([5, 6]) my_list ⇒ [1, 2, 3, 5, 6]
Inserting	list.insert(index, item)	my_list = [1, 2, 3] my_list.insert(1, "a") my_list ⇒ [1, "a", 2, 3]
Removing	list.remove(item)	my_list = [1, 2, 3] my_list.remove(2) my_list ⇒ [1, 3]
Removing	list.pop(index=-1)	my_list = [1, 2, 3] my_list.pop(1) returns 3 my_list ⇒ [1, 2]
Sorting	list.sort()	my_list = [3, 1, 2] my_list.sort() my_list ⇒ [1, 2, 3]
Reversing	list.reverse()	my_list.reverse() my_list ⇒ [3, 2, 1]
Comprehension	[expression for item in iterable condition]	[x**2 for x in range(5)] returns [0, 1, 4, 9, 16]

11.11   INTERACT WITH GENAI

Here are some questions and prompts you can interact with generative AI tools, including ChatGPT.

- Explain what a list is in Python. Why and how can a list contain different types of values?
- Discuss the different ways to create a list in Python. What are some common methods or functions used to generate lists?
- Describe how list slicing works in Python. How can you use slicing to access specific parts of a list?
- Generate an example of creating a list in Python with at least five elements. Demonstrate how to access the first, last, and a middle element using indexing.
- Provide an example of list slicing where you extract a sublist from an existing list. Show how slicing can be used to reverse a list as well.
- Illustrate how to manipulate a list by adding, removing, and modifying elements.
- Explain the concept of list comprehension in Python. How does it provide a more concise way to create lists?
- Provide an example of a list comprehension that generates a list of squares for numbers 1 through 10. Explain how it works compared to using a loop.
- Create a list comprehension that filters out all vowels from a given string and stores the remaining characters in a list. Show how this can be done in a single line of code.
- Submit a Python code snippet where you define, slice, and manipulate a list to AI and ask "Give me personalized feedback on the efficiency and readability of my list operations."
- Describe a challenge you faced when working with lists, such as accidentally modifying the original list when creating a copy to AI and ask AI for "Give me suggestions on how to avoid common pitfalls."

11.12   EXPLORE MORE OF LIST

At the end, here are the official documentations of the Python `list`:

- Brief introduction of list: https://docs.python.org/3/library/stdtypes.html#list
- More on lists: https://docs.python.org/3/tutorial/datastructures.html#more-on-lists

## CHAPTER 12

Tuple

How do you like `list` in Python? Is it powerful and convenient? In this chapter, we are going to learn a similar data structure, `tuple`. Lists and tuples are both used to store ordered collections of items, offering similar functionality like indexing and iteration. However, the key difference is that lists are mutable, allowing changes to their content, while tuples are immutable, making them safer for storing fixed data or as keys in dictionaries. Tuples are especially useful when you need lightweight, read-only containers that prioritize data integrity and performance.

Are you excited? Let's get started!

12.1 WHAT IS A TUPLE

12.1.1 Explanation

Why do we need tuples? Tuples are useful when you need to store a collection of objects that should not be modified, such as a database record or a geometric coordinate. Tuples are also useful when you need to return multiple values from a function.

Real-life examples:

- Coordinates: A tuple can represent a geographic coordinate, like (43.6532, -79.3832), which is the latitude and longitude of Toronto, Canada.
- Database Record: A tuple can represent a single record in a database, like (John, Smith, 25, New York), which could be a person's name, last name, age, and city.
- Product Information: A tuple can represent information about a product, like (Apple, iPhone, 128GB, $799), which could be the brand, model, storage size, and price of a phone.
- Time and Date: A tuple can represent a time and date, like (2024, 3, 15, 14, 30, 0), which could be the year, month, day, hour, minute, and second of a specific moment.

Remember, tuples are immutable, meaning they cannot be changed once created, so they are perfect for storing data that should not be modified.

12.2   CREATE A TUPLE

12.2.1   Demonstration

In Python, there are several methods for creating tuples, providing flexibility and convenience for different programming scenarios. One common method is to use the tuple constructor, `tuple()`, which initializes an empty tuple or converts another iterable object, such as a list, into a tuple.

```python
my_tuple_1 = tuple() # Create an empty tuple
print(my_tuple_1)
```

```
()
```

```python
my_tuple_2 = tuple([1, 2, 3]) # Create a tuple from a list
print(my_tuple_2)
```

```
(1, 2, 3)
```

```python
my_tuple_3 = tuple('Hello, world') # Create a tuple from a string
print(my_tuple_3)
```

```
('H', 'e', 'l', 'l', 'o', ',', ' ', 'w', 'o', 'r', 'l', 'd')
```

Another approach to creating tuples in Python is by direct assignment, where we manually specify the elements of the tuples within parentheses `()`.

```python
my_tuple_4 = () # Create an empty tuple
print(my_tuple_4)
```

```
()
```

```python
my_tuple_5 = (1, ) # Note the comma
print(my_tuple_5)
```

```
(1,)
```

```python
test = (1) # Note the comma
print(test, type(test))
```

```
1 <class 'int'>
```

```python
my_tuple_6 = (1, 2, 3) # Create a tuple
print(my_tuple_6)
```

```
(1, 2, 3)
```

```python
my_tuple_7 = tuple('Hello, world') # Create a tuple
print(my_tuple_7)
```

```
('H', 'e', 'l', 'l', 'o', ',', ' ', 'w', 'o', 'r', 'l', 'd')
```

In Python, the built-in function `len()` is used to determine the length or the number of elements in a tuple. When applied to a tuple, `len()` returns an integer representing the total count of elements contained within the tuple. This count includes all individual elements, regardless of their data type or complexity, providing a convenient way to quickly assess the length of the tuple.

```
print(my_tuple_1)
print(len(my_tuple_1)) # output 0
```

```
()
0
```

```
print(my_tuple_2)
print(len(my_tuple_2)) # output 3
```

```
(1, 2, 3)
3
```

```
print(my_tuple_3)
print(len(my_tuple_3)) # output 12
```

```
('H', 'e', 'l', 'l', 'o', ',', ' ', 'w', 'o', 'r', 'l', 'd')
12
```

```
print(my_tuple_4)
print(len(my_tuple_4)) # output 0
```

```
()
0
```

```
print(my_tuple_5)
print(len(my_tuple_5)) # output 1
```

```
(1,)
1
```

```
print(my_tuple_6)
print(len(my_tuple_6)) # output 3
```

```
(1, 2, 3)
3
```

12.2.2 Practice

Task: Create a tuple `tuple1` from a string `'Tuple Constructor'`. Print `tuple1` together with its length.

```
tuple1 = tuple('Tuple Constructor')
tuple1, len(tuple1)
```

```
(('T',
  'u',
  'p',
  'l',
  'e',
  ' ',
  'C',
  'o',
  'n',
```

```
    's',
    't',
    'r',
    'u',
    'c',
    't',
    'o',
    'r'),
 17)
```

Task: Create a tuple `tuple2` contains integers 5, 7. Print `tuple2` together with its length.

```
tuple2 = tuple([5, 7])
tuple2, len(tuple2)
```

`((5, 7), 2)`

Task: Create a tuple `tuple3` contains float 5.5, 5.2, and 5.0. Print `tuple3` together with its length.

```
tuple3 = tuple([5.5, 5.2, 5.0])
tuple3, len(tuple3)
```

`((5.5, 5.2, 5.0), 3)`

Task: Create a tuple `tuple4` contains string `'Apple'` and `'Pear'`. Print `tuple4` together with its length.

```
tuple4 = ('Apple', 'Pear')
tuple4, len(tuple4)
```

`(('Apple', 'Pear'), 2)`

12.3 HETEROGENEOUS TUPLE IN PYTHON

12.3.1 Demonstration

Similar to a list tuple in Python may contain elements of different data types. This means that a tuple can contain a mix of strings, integers, floats, Booleans, and other data types.

```
# Creating a heterogeneous tuple
my_tuple_7 = ('Apple', 5, 5.5, True)

# Displaying the tuple
print(my_tuple_7)
```

`('Apple', 5, 5.5, True)`

```
my_tuple_8 = [my_tuple_1, my_tuple_2, my_tuple_5, my_tuple_7, 4]
print(my_tuple_8)
```

`[(), (1, 2, 3), (1,), ('Apple', 5, 5.5, True), 4]`

Note: The `len()` counts the number of elements in a tuple. If the element is another tuple, it is still counted as 1.

```
print(my_tuple_7)
print(len(my_tuple_7)) # output 4
```

```
('Apple', 5, 5.5, True)
4
```

```
print(my_tuple_8)
print(len(my_tuple_8)) # output 5
```

```
[(), (1, 2, 3), (1,), ('Apple', 5, 5.5, True), 4]
5
```

12.3.2 Practice

Task: Create a tuple `tuple5` containing some numbers (combination of int and float). Print `tuple5` together with its length.

```
tuple5 = (2.1, 5.2, 3, 4, 1)
print(tuple5, len(tuple5))
```

```
(2.1, 5.2, 3, 4, 1) 5
```

Task: Create a tuple `tuple6` containing the following values:

1. customer name (`str`)
2. product name (`str`)
3. product price (`float`)
4. product quantity (`int`)
5. aid_status (`bool`).

Print `tuple6` together with its length.

```
tuple6 = ('Neo', 'iPhone', 999.99, 2, True)
print(tuple6, len(tuple6))
```

```
('Neo', 'iPhone', 999.99, 2, True) 5
```

12.4 ACCESS ELEMENTS IN A TUPLE BY INDEX

12.4.1 Demonstration

In Python, accessing elements in a tuple is similar to list by using indices, which represent the positions of the elements within the tuple. The first element of the tuple is at index 0, the second element is at index 1, and so on. It's important to note that the index of the last element in a tuple is always one less than the length of the tuple. For example, if a tuple has 5 elements, the last element is at index `len(tuple) - 1`. Attempting to access an index larger than `len(tuple) - 1` will result in an error, as it exceeds the bounds of the tuple.

```
# Define a tuple of fruits

my_tuple_9 = ('apple', 'banana', 'orange')

print(my_tuple_9, len(my_tuple_9))
```

('apple', 'banana', 'orange') 3

```
# Accessing the first element
print(my_tuple_9[0])  # Output: 'apple'
```

apple

```
# Accessing the third element
print(my_tuple_9[2])  # Output: 'orange'
```

orange

```
# Accessing the last element
print(my_tuple_9[len(my_tuple_9) - 1])  # Output: 'orange'
```

orange

```
# Attempting to access an index larger than len(tuple) - 1
# This will result in an IndexError
print(my_tuple_9[3])  # IndexError: tuple index out of range
```

```
---------------------------------------------------------------------
IndexError                              Traceback (most recent call last)
<ipython-input-39-13a04768eac3> in <cell line: 3>()
     1 # Attempting to access an index larger than len(tuple) - 1
     2 # This will result in an IndexError
----> 3 print(my_tuple_9[3])  # IndexError: list index out of range

IndexError: tuple index out of range
```

Similar to lists, tuples support negative indexing as well. It provides a convenient way to access elements relative to the end of the tuple without needing to calculate the exact index.

```
# Accessing the last element using negative index
print(my_tuple_9[-1])  # Output: 'orange'
```

orange

```
# Accessing the second-to-last element using negative index
print(my_tuple_9[-2])  # Output: 'banana'
```

banana

```
# Accessing the third-to-last element using negative index
print(my_tuple_9[-3])  # Output: 'apple'
```

apple

```
# Attempting to access an index beyond the range of negative indices
# This will result in an IndexError
print(my_tuple_9[-6])  # IndexError: tuple index out of range
```

```
-------------------------------------------------------------------------
IndexError                                Traceback (most recent call last)
<ipython-input-44-92ffb58201d5> in <cell line: 3>()
      1 # Attempting to access an index beyond the range of negative indices
      2 # This will result in an IndexError
----> 3 print(my_tuple_9[-6])  # IndexError: tuple index out of range

IndexError: tuple index out of range
```

12.4.2 Practice

```
# Run this cell for these practice
tuple_practice = (2, 4, 6, 8, 10)
```

Task: Print the first element in `tuple_practice` using non-negative index.

```
tuple_practice[0]
```

2

Task: Print the 2nd element in `tuple_practice` using non-negative index.

```
tuple_practice[1]
```

4

Task: Print the 3rd element in `tuple_practice` using non-negative index.

```
tuple_practice[2]
```

6

Task: Print the last element in `tuple_practice` using non-negative index.

```
tuple_practice[len(tuple_practice)-1]
```

10

Task: Print the last element in `tuple_practice` using negative index.

```
tuple_practice[-1]
```

10

Task: Print the first element in `tuple_practice` using negative index.

```
tuple_practice[-len(tuple_practice)]
```

2

Task: Find a positive index that will result an error.

```
tuple_practice[5]
```

```
-----------------------------------------------------------------------
IndexError                              Traceback (most recent call last)
<ipython-input-16-66ec6c0b5a7f> in <cell line: 1>()
----> 1 tuple_practice[5]

IndexError: tuple index out of range
```

Task: find a negative index that will result an error.

```
tuple_practice[-6]
```

```
-----------------------------------------------------------------------
IndexError                              Traceback (most recent call last)
<ipython-input-17-b05be02acf7a> in <cell line: 1>()
----> 1 tuple_practice[-6]

IndexError: tuple index out of range
```

12.5   ACCESS ELEMENTS IN A TUPLE BY ITERATION

12.5.1   Demonstration

Iterating through a Python tuple allows for the sequential processing of each element within the tuple. One common method of iteration involves using indices to access elements individually, where a loop iterates over the indices of the tuple and accesses each element using its corresponding index.

Using a for loop to iterate directly over the elements of a tuple simplifies the iteration process by abstracting away the index management. This approach is often preferred in Python for its readability and simplicity.

```python
# Define a tuple of numbers
numbers = (1, 2, 3, 4, 5)

# Iterate using index-based iteration
for i in range(len(numbers)):
    print(numbers[i])   # Accessing elements using index

# Iterate using direct iteration
for num in numbers:
    print(num)   # Accessing elements directly
```

```
1
2
3
4
5
1
2
3
4
5
```

In these examples, we iterate through the tuple numbers using both index-based iteration and direct iteration approaches. In the index-based iteration, we use a for loop to iterate over the indices of the tuple and access each element using its corresponding index. In contrast, the direct iteration approach simplifies the process by directly iterating over the elements of the tuple, eliminating the need for index manipulation. This results in cleaner and more concise code, enhancing readability and reducing potential errors.

12.5.2 Practice

```
# Run this cell for this practice
numbers = (1, 2, 2, 3, 5)
```

Task: Print each element in **numbers** on a new line using a for loop for iteration.

```
for i in numbers:
    print(i)
```

```
1
2
2
3
5
```

Task: Calculate the sum in **numbers** using a for loop for iteration and print the sum.

```
total = 0
for i in numbers:
    total += i
print(total)
```

```
13
```

Task: Count how many 2 in **numbers** using a for loop for iteration and print the count.

```
count_2 = 0
for i in numbers:
    if i == 2:
        count_2 += 1
print(count_2)
```

```
2
```

Task: Count the number of odd integers in **numbers** using a for loop for iteration and print the count.

```
count_odd = 0
for i in numbers:
    if i %2 != 0:
        count_odd += 1
print(count_odd)
```

```
3
```

12.6 SLICE A TUPLE

12.6.1 Demonstration

Similar to list, slicing tuples in Python allows for the extraction of a subset of elements from a tuple using a specified range of indices. When using non-negative indices, slicing involves specifying the starting index, ending index (exclusive), and an optional step size. The syntax for slicing is `tuple[start:end:step]`, where `start` indicates the index of the first element to include, `end` indicates the index after the last element to include, and `step` determines the increment between consecutive indices. If any of these parameters are omitted, default values are used: `start` defaults to 0, `end` defaults to the length of the tuple, and `step` defaults to 1.

```python
# Define a tuple of numbers
numbers = (0, 1, 2, 3, 4, 5, 6, 7, 8, 9)
```

```python
# Slicing with non-negative indices
print(numbers[0:5])      # Output: (0, 1, 2, 3, 4)
```

```
(0, 1, 2, 3, 4)
```

```python
print(numbers[:5])       # Output: (0, 1, 2, 3, 4)
```

```
(0, 1, 2, 3, 4)
```

```python
print(numbers[3:11])       # Output: (3, 4, 5, 6, 7, 8, 9)
```

```
(3, 4, 5, 6, 7, 8, 9)
```

```python
print(numbers[3:])       # Output: (3, 4, 5, 6, 7, 8, 9)
```

```
(3, 4, 5, 6, 7, 8, 9)
```

```python
print(numbers[::2])      # Output: (0, 2, 4, 6, 8)
```

```
(0, 2, 4, 6, 8)
```

```python
print(numbers[3:8:3])    # Output: (3, 6)
```

```
(3, 6)
```

We can also utilize the negative indices as we did to lists.

```python
# Slicing with negative indices
print(numbers[-5:])      # Output: (5, 6, 7, 8, 9)
```

```
(5, 6, 7, 8, 9)
```

```python
print(numbers[:-5])      # Output: (0, 1, 2, 3, 4)
```

```
(0, 1, 2, 3, 4)
```

```python
print(numbers[::-1])     # Output: (9, 8, 7, 6, 5, 4, 3, 2, 1, 0)
```

```
(9, 8, 7, 6, 5, 4, 3, 2, 1, 0)
```

Combining both non-negative and negative indices in slicing provides a powerful mechanism for extracting subsets of elements from Python lists with flexibility and precision.

```
# Define a tuple of letters
letters = tuple('Python')
print(letters, len(letters))
```

('P', 'y', 't', 'h', 'o', 'n') 6

```
# Slicing with a combination of non-negative and negative indices
print(letters[2:-2])      # Output: ('t', 'h')
```

('t', 'h')

```
print(letters[-2:6])      # Output: ('o', 'n')
```

('o', 'n')

```
print(letters[1:-1:2])    # Output: ('y', 'h')
```

('y', 'h')

```
print(letters[-6:3])      # Output: ('P', 'y', 't')
```

('P', 'y', 't')

```
print(letters[::2])       # Output: ('P', 't', 'o')
```

('P', 't', 'o')

```
print(letters[:1:-1])     # Output: ('n', 'o', 'h', 't')
```

('n', 'o', 'h', 't')

12.6.2 Practice

```
# Define students and run it for this practice
students = ('Alice', 'Bobby', 'Cathy', 'David', 'Ethan', 'Frank')
```

Task: Extract the first three students from the tuple **students** using slicing with non-negative indices.

```
students[:3]
```

('Alice', 'Bobby', 'Cathy')

Task: Extract the last three students from the tuple **students** using slicing with non-negative indices.

```
students[-3:]
```

('David', 'Ethan', 'Frank')

Task: Extract the middle two students from the tuple **students** using slicing with non-negative indices.

```
students[2:-2]
```

```
('Cathy', 'David')
```

Task: Create a new tuple called **team1** containing every other students from the tuple **students** using slicing with non-negative indices.

```
team1 = students[::2]
team1
```

```
('Alice', 'Cathy', 'Ethan')
```

Task: Create a new tuple called **team2** containing every one from three students from the tuple **students** using slicing with non-negative indices.

```
team2 = students[::3]
team2
```

```
('Alice', 'David')
```

Task: Reverse the order of elements in the tuple **students** using slicing with negative indices.

```
students[::-1]
```

```
('Frank', 'Ethan', 'David', 'Cathy', 'Bobby', 'Alice')
```

12.7 TUPLE COMPREHENSION

12.7.1 Demonstration

Tuple comprehension, similar to list comprehension, provides a compact and readable way to generate tuples using an expression and an optional for loop. The syntax for tuple comprehension is enclosed within parentheses **tuple()** instead of square brackets **[]**.

The general syntax is:

```
tuple_variable = tuple(expression for item in iterable condition)
```

```
# Using tuple comprehension to generate a tuple of squares
squares_tuple = tuple(x ** 2 for x in range(1, 6))
print('Tuple of squares:', squares_tuple)
```

```
Tuple of squares: (1, 4, 9, 16, 25)
```

```
# Using tuple comprehension to filter odd numbers from a list
numbers = [1, 2, 3, 4, 5]
odd_numbers_tuple = tuple(x for x in numbers if x % 2 != 0)
print('Tuple of odd numbers:', odd_numbers_tuple)
```

```
Tuple of odd numbers: (1, 3, 5)
```

```
# Using tuple comprehension to create a tuple of tuples
nested_list = [(1, 2), (3, 4), (5, 6)]
```

```
flattened_tuple = tuple(item for t in nested_list for item in t)
print('Tuple of tuples:', flattened_tuple)
```

Tuple of tuples: (1, 2, 3, 4, 5, 6)

```
# Using tuple comprehension to create a tuple of strings
words = ['apple', 'banana', 'cherry']
uppercase_tuple = tuple(word.upper() for word in words)
print('Tuple of uppercase words:', uppercase_tuple)
```

Tuple of uppercase words: ('APPLE', 'BANANA', 'CHERRY')

12.7.2　Practice

```
# Define students and run it for this practice
students = ['Alice', 'Ann', 'Anny', 'Bob', 'Bobby', 'Bubbi']
```

Task: Using tuple comprehension, put all names in `students` to a tuple `line1`.

```
line1 = tuple(s for s in students)
line1
```

('Alice', 'Ann', 'Anny', 'Bob', 'Bobby', 'Bubbi')

Task: Using tuple comprehension, put all names that starts `'A'` in `students` to a tuple `line2`.

```
line2 = tuple(s for s in students if s[0] == 'A')
line2
```

('Alice', 'Ann', 'Anny')

Task: Using tuple comprehension, put all names that ends with `'y'` in `students` to a tuple `line3`.

```
line3 = tuple(s for s in students if s[-1] == 'y')
line3
```

('Anny', 'Bobby')

Task: Using tuple comprehension, put all names that have less than four letters in `students` to a tuple `line4`.

```
line4 = tuple(s for s in students if len(s) < 4)
line4
```

('Ann', 'Bob')

Task: Using tuple comprehension, put the pairs of all students in `students` to a tuple `pairs`.

```
pairs = tuple((a, b) for a in students for b in students)
pairs
```

(('Alice', 'Alice'),
 ('Alice', 'Ann'),
 ('Alice', 'Anny'),

```
...eliminated to save space...
 ('Bubbi', 'Bob'),
 ('Bubbi', 'Bobby'),
 ('Bubbi', 'Bubbi'))
```

Task: Using tuple comprehension, put the pairs of all students in `students` to a tuple `pairs` with the condition:

1. The student will be be paired with another student. For example, `'Ann'` won't be paired with `'Ann'`
2. Students will be paired with names starting with same letter. `'Ann'` will be paired with `'Anny'` but not `'Bob'`.

```
pairs = tuple((a, b) for a in students for b in students if a != b and a[0] == b[0])
pairs
```

```
((('Alice', 'Ann'),
 ('Alice', 'Anny'),
 ('Ann', 'Alice'),
...eliminated to save space...
 ('Bobby', 'Bubbi'),
 ('Bubbi', 'Bob'),
 ('Bubbi', 'Bobby'))
```

Here, let's summarize what we learned about `tuple` in Table 12.1.

Table 12.1 Summary of Python tuples.

Feature	Syntax	Examples
Creation	`()` or `tuple()`	`my_tuple = (1, 2, 3)` `my_tuple = tuple([1, 2, 3])`
Accessing	`tuple[index]`	`my_tuple[0]` returns 1 `my_tuple[-1]` returns 3
Slicing	`tuple[start:stop:step]`	`my_tuple[1:3]` returns `(2, 3)` `my_tuple[::2]` returns `(1, 3)`
Immutability	Tuples cannot be changed after creation.	`my_tuple[0]` = 5 raises `TypeError`.
Packing	Use a sequence of values to create a tuple without parentheses.	`my_tuple = 1, 2, 3` `my_tuple` is `(1, 2, 3)`
Unpacking	Assign tuple elements to multiple variables.	`my_tuple = (1, 2, 3)` `a, b, c = my_tuple` assigns a=1, b=2, c=3.
Searching	`tuple.index(item)`	`my_tuple.index(2)` returns 1.
Counting	`tuple.count(item)`	`my_tuple.count(2)` returns 1 if 2 appears once.

12.8 INTERACT WITH GENAI

Here are some questions and prompts you can interact with generative AI tools, including ChatGPT.

- Explain what a tuple is in Python. How does it differ from a list, and why might you choose to use a tuple instead?
- Discuss the concept of immutability in tuples. Why can't you modify a tuple after it has been created?
- Describe how tuples can be used for returning multiple values from a function or for grouping related data.
- Generate an example of creating a tuple in Python with at least three elements. Demonstrate how to access individual elements using indexing.
- Provide an example of tuple unpacking, where you assign the elements of a tuple to separate variables in a single line of code.
- Illustrate how tuples can be used in a function that returns multiple values, such as returning both the quotient and remainder from a division operation.
- Reflect on the situations where using a tuple is more appropriate than using a list. How does the immutability of tuples contribute to code safety and reliability?
- Consider a project where you used tuples to store data. How did the choice of tuples impact the structure and functionality of your code?
- Submit a Python code snippet where you define and use a tuple. Receive personalized feedback on the tuple's usage and any potential improvements in your approach.
- Describe a challenge you faced when working with tuples, such as needing to modify a tuple. Ask AI to explain how to work around tuple immutability or when to consider using a different data structure.

12.9 EXPLORE MORE OF TUPLE

At the end, here are the official documentations of Python `tuple`:

- Brief introduction of tuple: https://docs.python.org/3/library/stdtypes.html#tuples
- More on tuples: https://docs.python.org/3/tutorial/datastructures.html#tuples-and-sequences

## CHAPTER 13

Set

N ow we have learned `list` and `tuple` in Python. Both of them are array-like data structures. In this chapter, we are going to learn a mapping-based data structure, `set`. sets are unordered and only hold distinct elements, automatically eliminating duplicates. Unlike lists and tuples, sets don't support indexing or slicing but do well in operations like union, intersection, and difference. This makes sets an ideal choice when managing collections where uniqueness and membership tests are priorities, such as removing duplicates or checking for common elements. Are you excited? Let's get started!

13.1 WHAT IS A SET

13.1.1 Explanation

A set in Python is an unordered collection of unique elements. It is defined by enclosing its elements within curly braces {} (which is the same as the dictionary we are going to learn later). Sets are mutable, meaning you can add or remove elements from them, but they do not support indexing or slicing like lists or tuples.

Sets offer several advantages and use cases in Python programming. Sets ensure that each element appears only once, making them ideal for removing duplicates from a collection. Sets provide an efficient way to check for membership, that is, whether an element exists in the set or not. Sets support mathematical set operations such as union, intersection, difference, and symmetric difference, making them useful for tasks involving comparisons between collections.

13.1.2 Practice

Task: Can you list 3 applications in your real-life that utilize the concept of sets?

DOI: 10.1201/9781003527725-13

13.2 CREATE A SET

13.2.1 Demonstration

You can create a set using various ways like we did for list and tuple. The first approach is using the `set()` constructor and passing an iterable containing the elements of the set. Note that if there are duplicate values in the iterable, duplicates will be removed.

```python
# Creating an empty set using the set() constructor
my_set = set()
print('Set created using set() constructor', my_set)
```

Set created using set() constructor set()

```python
# Creating a set using the set() constructor and a list
my_list = [1, 2, 2, 3, 3]
my_set = set(my_list)
print('Set created using set() constructor and a list:', my_set)
```

Set created using set() constructor and a list: {1, 2, 3}

```python
# Creating a set using the set() constructor and a tuple
my_tuple = (1, 2, 2, 3, 3)
my_set = set(my_tuple)
print('Set created using set() constructor and a tuple:', my_set)
```

Set created using set() constructor and a tuple: {1, 2, 3}

Another approach to creating sets in Python is by direct assignment, using curly braces {} and elements. Note that since set and dictionary both use {}, if you are going to create an empty set, you must use `set()`. Using {} without elements will create a dictionary not a set.

```python
# {} with no elements is a dictionary
example = {}
type(example)
```

dict

```python
# Creating a set using curly braces and unique elements
my_set = {1, 2, 3}
print('Set created using curly braces:', my_set)
```

Set created using curly braces: {1, 2, 3}

```python
# Creating a set using curly braces and duplicate elements
my_set = {1, 2, 2, 3, 3}
print('Set created using curly braces:', my_set)
```

Set created using curly braces: {1, 2, 3}

In Python, the `len()` function is used to determine the number of elements in a collection (such as list, tuple, etc.) When applied to a set, it returns the count of unique elements present in the set. The `len()` function provides a convenient way to obtain the size of a set, allowing you to perform various operations and checks based on the number of elements present in the set.

```python
# Creating a set
my_set = {1, 2, 3, 4, 5}

# Using the len() function to get the number of elements in the set
set_length = len(my_set)

print('Number of elements in the set:', set_length)
```

Number of elements in the set: 5

```python
# Creating a set
my_set = {1, 2, 3,0, 'a', 4, True}

# Using the len() function to get the number of elements in the set
set_length = len(my_set)

print('Number of elements in the set:', set_length)
```

Number of elements in the set: 6

13.2.2 Practice

Task: Create a set `set1` from a string 'set Constructor'. Print the set together with its length.

```python
set1 = set('Set Constructor')
print(set1, len(set1))
```

{'o', 'u', 'C', 'S', 'c', 'r', ' ', 't', 's', 'n', 'e'} 11

Task: Create a set `set2` from a list of numbers [3, 0, 2, 1, 0, 2, 1]. Print the set together with its length.

```python
set2 = set([3, 0, 2, 1, 0, 2, 1])
print(set2, len(set2))
```

{0, 1, 2, 3} 4

Task: Create a set `set3` from a list of students, ['Aaron', 'Ann', 'Aaron', 'Brian', 'Cathy', 'Ann', 'Brian'].

```python
set3 = set(['Aaron', 'Ann', 'Aaron', 'Brian', 'Cathy', 'Ann', 'Brian'])
print(set3, len(set3))
```

{'Cathy', 'Brian', 'Ann', 'Aaron'} 4

13.3   ELEMENTS IN A SET

13.3.1   Demonstration

In Python, sets are unordered collections of unique elements, which means they do not support indexing or slicing like lists or tuples. However, you can still access elements in a set using different methods.

```python
# Creating a set
my_set = {1, 2, 3, 4, 5}

# Accessing elements using a for loop
for element in my_set:
    print(element)
```

```
1
2
3
4
5
```

```python
# Creating a set
my_set = {1, 2, 3, 4, 5}

# Checking if an element exists in the set
if 3 in my_set:
    print('Element 3 exists in the set')
else:
    print('Element 3 does not exist in the set')
```

```
Element 3 exists in the set
```

```python
# Creating a set
my_set = {1, 2, 3, 4, 5}

# Converting set to list and accessing elements by index
set_list = list(my_set)
print("First element:", set_list[0])
print("Second element:", set_list[1])
```

```
First element: 1
Second element: 2
```

13.3.2   Practice

Task: Print out all elements in set1.

```python
for s in set1:
  print(s)
```

```
o
u
C
S
c
```

r

t

s

n

e

Task: Check if 5 is in `set2`.

```
print(5 in set2)
```

`False`

Task: With attended list as `['Aaron', 'Amed', 'Ann', 'Brian', 'David']`, print out if they are in `set3`

```
for a in ['Aaron', 'Amed', 'Ann', 'Brian', 'David']:
  if a in set3:
    print(f'{a} is in set3.')
  else:
    print(f'{a} is not in set3.')
```

```
Aaron is in set3.
Amed is not in set3.
Ann is in set3.
Brian is in set3.
David is not in set3.
```

Task: Convert `set3` to a list `list3`, and print the first element of `list3`.

```
list3 = list(set3)
print(list3[0])
```

`Cathy`

13.4   SET OPERATIONS

13.4.1   Demonstration

Set operations in Python involve various mathematical operations that can be performed on sets. These operations include union, intersection, difference, symmetric difference, and subset testing.

Union (| or `union()`): The union of two sets A and B contains all unique elements from both sets.

```
# Example of union operation
set1 = {1, 2, 3}
set2 = {3, 4, 5}

# Using the | operator
union_result = set1 | set2
print('Union using | operator:', union_result)
```

```
# Using the union() method
union_result = set1.union(set2)
print('Union using union() method:', union_result)
```

```
Union using | operator: {1, 2, 3, 4, 5}
Union using union() method: {1, 2, 3, 4, 5}
```

Intersection (& or `ntersection()`): The intersection of two sets A and B contains only elements that are common to both sets.

```
# Example of intersection operation
set1 = {1, 2, 3}
set2 = {3, 4, 5}

# Using the & operator
intersection_result = set1 & set2
print('Intersection using & operator:', intersection_result)

# Using the intersection() method
intersection_result = set1.intersection(set2)
print('Intersection using intersection() method:', intersection_result)
```

```
Intersection using & operator: {3}
Intersection using intersection() method: {3}
```

Difference (- or `difference()`): The difference between two sets A and B contains elements that are in A but not in B. Note that the difference operation is directional, A - B may be different than B - A.

```
# Example of difference operation
set1 = {1, 2, 3}
set2 = {3, 4, 5}

# Using the - operator
difference_result1 = set1 - set2
print('Difference using - operator from set1:', difference_result1)

# Using the difference() method
difference_result1 = set1.difference(set2)
print('Difference using difference() method from set1:', difference_result1)

# Using the - operator
difference_result2 = set2 - set1
print('Difference using - operator from set2:', difference_result2)

# Using the difference() method
difference_result2 = set2.difference(set1)
print('Difference using difference() method from set2:', difference_result2)
```

```
Difference using - operator from set1: {1, 2}
Difference using difference() method from set1: {1, 2}
Difference using - operator from set2: {4, 5}
Difference using difference() method from set2: {4, 5}
```

Subset and Superset Testing (<= and >=): You can test whether one set is a subset or superset of another using the <= and >= operators, respectively.

```
# Example of subset and superset testing
set1 = {1, 2, 3, 4}
set2 = {2, 3}

# Subset testing
if set2 <= set1:
    print('set2 is a subset of set1')
else:
    print('set2 is not a subset of set1')

# Superset testing
if set1 >= set2:
    print('set1 is a superset of set2')
else:
    print('set1 is not a superset of set2')
```

```
set2 is a subset of set1
set1 is a superset of set2
```

13.4.2 Practice

```
# run this cell for this practice
set1 = {'Apple', 'Banana', 'Cherry'}
set2 = {'Blueberry', 'Cherry', 'Raspberry', 'Blackberry'}
```

Task: Create the union of `set1` and `set2` as `set_union`. Print the `set_union` as well as it's length.

```
set_union = set1 | set2
print(set_union, len(set_union))
```

```
{'Cherry', 'Apple', 'Blackberry', 'Blueberry', 'Banana', 'Raspberry'} 6
```

Task: Create the intersection of `set1` and `set2` as `set_intersect`. Print the `set_intersect` as well as it's length.

```
set_intersect = set1 & set2
print(set_intersect, len(set_intersect))
```

```
{'Cherry'} 1
```

Task: Create the difference from `set1` to `set2` as `set1_2`. Print the `set1_2` as well as it's length.

```
set1_2 = set1 - set2
print(set1_2, len(set1_2))
```

```
{'Banana', 'Apple'} 2
```

Task: Create the difference from `set2` to `set1` as `set2_1`. Print the `set2_1` as well as it's length.

```
set2_1 = set2 - set1
print(set2_1, len(set2_1))
```

```
{'Blueberry', 'Blackberry', 'Raspberry'} 3
```

Task: Check if `set_union` is a superset of `set1`.

```
print(set_union >= set1)
```
True

Task: Check if `set_intersect` is a subset of `set2`.

```
print(set_intersect <= set2)
```
True

Task: Check if `set2_1` is a subset of `set_intersect`.

```
print(set2_1 <= set_intersect)
```
False

Task: Check if `set2_1` is a superset of `set_intersect`.

```
print(set1_2 >= set_intersect)
```
False

13.5   SET METHODS

13.5.1   Demonstration

Set methods provide convenient ways to manipulate sets in Python, allowing you to add, remove, and update elements efficiently. Understanding how to use these methods will help you effectively work with sets in your Python programs.

`add()`: Adds an element to the set if it is not already present.

```
my_set = {1, 2, 3}
my_set.add(4)
print(my_set)  # Output: {1, 2, 3, 4}
```
{1, 2, 3, 4}

```
# If you add an element that is in the set already, it will be ignored
my_set.add(4)
print(my_set)  # Output: {1, 2, 3, 4}
```
{1, 2, 3, 4}

`remove()`: Removes the specified element from the set. Raises a `KeyError` if the element is not present.

```
my_set = {1, 2, 3}
my_set.remove(2)
print(my_set)  # Output: {1, 3}
```
{1, 3}

```
# If you remove 2 again, a KeyError will be raised
my_set.remove(2)
print(my_set)  # Output: {1, 3}
```

```
--------------------------------------------------------------------
KeyError                              Traceback (most recent call last)
<ipython-input-27-cbfac0215b21> in <cell line: 2>()
      1 # If you remove 2 again, a KeyError will be raised
----> 2 my_set.remove(2)
      3 print(my_set)  # Output: {1, 3}

KeyError: 2
```

discard(): Removes the specified element from the set if it is present. Does not raise any error if the element is not present. It works as a safer remove().

```
my_set = {1, 2, 3}
my_set.discard(2)
print(my_set)  # Output: {1, 3}
```

```
{1, 3}
```

```
# remove 2 again won't raise KeyError
my_set.discard(2)
print(my_set)  # Output: {1, 3}
```

```
{1, 3}
```

update(): Adds elements from another iterable (e.g., list, set) to the set.

```
my_set = {1, 2, 3}
my_set.update([4, 5, 6])
print(my_set)  # Output: {1, 2, 3, 4, 5, 6}
```

```
{1, 2, 3, 4, 5, 6}
```

clear(): Removes all elements from the set.

```
my_set = {1, 2, 3}
my_set.clear()
print(my_set)  # Output: set()
```

```
set()
```

13.5.2 Practice

```
# Run this cell for this practice
set1 = {'Apple', 'Banana', 'Cherry'}
set2 = {'Blueberry', 'Cherry', 'Raspberry', 'Blackberry'}
```

Task: Add 'Kiwi' to set1. Print the set1 as well as it's length.

```
set1.add('Kiwi')
print(set1, len(set1))
```

```
{'Cherry', 'Banana', 'Kiwi', 'Apple'} 4
```

Task: Remove `'Kiwi'` from `set1`. Print the `set1` as well as it's length.

```
set1.remove('Kiwi')
print(set1, len(set1))
```

{'Cherry', 'Banana', 'Apple'} 3

Task: Remove `'Pear'` to `set1` using `remove()`. Print the `set1` as well as it's length.

```
set1.remove('Pear')
print(set1, len(set1))
```

```
---------------------------------------------------------------------
KeyError                              Traceback (most recent call last)
<ipython-input-60-aef58cd0dfda> in <cell line: 1>()
----> 1 set1.remove('Pear')
      2 print(set1, len(set1))

KeyError: 'Pear'
```

Task: Remove `'Pear'` to `set1` using `discard()`. Print the `set1` as well as it's length.

```
set1.discard('Pear')
print(set1, len(set1))
```

{'Cherry', 'Banana', 'Apple'} 3

Task: Update `set1` with `set2`. Print both `set1` and `set2` after the update.

```
set1.update(set2)
print(set1, len(set1))
print(set2, len(set2))
```

{'Blackberry', 'Banana', 'Raspberry', 'Cherry', 'Apple', 'Blueberry'} 6
{'Blueberry', 'Blackberry', 'Raspberry', 'Cherry'} 4

Task: Clear `set2`. Print the `set2` as well as it's length.

```
set2.clear()
print(set2, len(set2))
```

set() 0

13.6 SET COMPREHENSION

13.6.1 Demonstration

Python also supports set comprehension, which allows for the creation of sets using a concise and efficient syntax similar to list and tuple comprehensions. Set comprehension generates sets by applying an expression to each item in an iterable, enclosed within curly braces {}.

The general syntax is:

```
set_variable = {expression for item in iterable condition}
```

```
# Using set comprehension to generate a set of squares
squares_set = {x ** 2 for x in range(1, 6)}
print('Set of squares:', squares_set)
```

Set of squares: {1, 4, 9, 16, 25}

```
# Using set comprehension to filter odd numbers from a list
numbers = [1, 2, 3, 3, 4, 5, 5]
odd_numbers_set = {x for x in numbers if x % 2 != 0}
print('Set of odd numbers:', odd_numbers_set) # Duplicates will be removed
```

Set of odd numbers: {1, 3, 5}

```
# Using set comprehension to create a set of first characters from words
words = ['apple', 'banana', 'cherry']
first_characters_set = {word[0] for word in words}
print('Set of first characters:', first_characters_set)
```

Set of first characters: {'c', 'b', 'a'}

```
# Using set comprehension to create a set of unique intergers
import random

unique_numbers = {random.randint(0, 10) for i in range(10)}
print('Set of random integers:', unique_numbers)
```

Set of random integers: {0, 2, 4, 6, 7, 8, 9, 10}

Here, let's summarize what we learned about the **set** in Table 13.1.

Table 13.1 Summary of Python sets.

Feature	Syntax	Examples
Creation	{} or set()	my_set = {1, 2, 3} my_set = set([1, 2, 3])
Access	Sets are unordered and do not support indexing.	for x in my_set
Add	set.add(item)	my_set.add(4) my_set ⇒ {1, 2, 3, 4}
Update	set.update(iterable)	my_set.update([4, 5]) my_set ⇒ {1, 2, 3, 4, 5}
Remove	set.remove(item) set.discard(item)	my_set.remove(2) my_set ⇒ {1, 3} my_set.discard(10) does nothing if 10 is not present.
Membership	item in set	2 in my_set returns True.

13.7 INTERACT WITH GENAI

Here are some questions and prompts you can interact with generative AI tools, including ChatGPT.

- Explain what a set is in Python. How does it differ from other data structures like lists and tuples?
- Discuss the properties of sets, such as uniqueness and unordered elements. Why are these properties important?
- Describe common use cases for sets, such as removing duplicates from a list or performing mathematical set operations.
- Generate an example of creating a set in Python with at least five elements. Demonstrate how to add and remove elements using methods like `add()` and `remove()`.
- Provide an example of using set operations such as union, intersection, and difference. Show how these operations can be used to compare two sets.
- Illustrate how to convert a list with duplicate elements into a set to remove duplicates and then convert it back to a list.
- Reflect on the advantages of using sets in Python. How does the ability to store unique elements and perform fast membership checks benefit your programs?
- Consider a situation where you used sets to handle data. How did the properties of sets, such as immutability and uniqueness, influence your approach?
- Submit a Python code snippet where you define and manipulate a set. Receive personalized feedback on the effectiveness and efficiency of your set operations.
- Describe a challenge you faced when working with sets, such as trying to access elements by index or dealing with unordered elements. Ask AI to suggest alternative approaches or ways to better utilize sets.

13.8   EXPLORE MORE OF SET

At the end, here are the official documentations of Python `set`:

- Brief introduction of sets: https://docs.python.org/3/library/stdtypes.html#set
- More on sets: https://docs.python.org/3/tutorial/datastructures.html#sets

## CHAPTER 14

Dictionary

W HILE `set` stores unique, unordered elements, Python `dict` allows you to associate each element with a unique key, creating key-value pairs. Unlike sets, dictionaries provide a way to access values efficiently using keys, making them ideal for situations where quick lookups or data associations are needed. This makes dictionaries a powerful tool for tasks such as storing configurations, counting occurrences, or representing relationships between data. Are you ready? Let's get started!

14.1 WHAT IS A DICTIONARY

14.1.1 Explanation

Dictionaries in Python employ a mapping mechanism that associates unique keys with corresponding values. Unlike sequences such as lists or tuples, which use positional indexing, dictionaries utilize keys to access and retrieve values. This mapping mechanism enables efficient storage, retrieval, and manipulation of key-value pairs within the dictionary data structure.

Internally, dictionaries in Python utilize hash tables to implement the mapping mechanism. Hash tables provide constant-time average-case complexity for operations such as insertion, retrieval, and deletion, making dictionaries highly efficient for storing and accessing data. Hashing allows Python to quickly compute the memory location associated with a given key, facilitating fast lookups even for large dictionaries.

Dictionaries play a crucial role in Python programming due to their versatility and efficiency. They offer a convenient way to organize and manipulate data using meaningful key-value pairs, allowing for intuitive data representation and access. Dictionaries are widely used in various programming tasks, including data processing, configuration management, caching, and more.

Dictionaries find applications in numerous real-life scenarios. Dictionaries are often used to represent database records, where each key corresponds to a field name, and the associated value represents the field's value. Dictionaries are used to store

DOI: 10.1201/9781003527725-14

configuration settings for software applications, with keys representing configuration parameters and values representing their respective values. Dictionaries serve as efficient caching mechanisms, storing previously computed results with keys representing input parameters and values representing the corresponding output. Dictionaries are employed in language translation systems, where keys represent words or phrases in one language, and values represent their translations in another language. Dictionaries are used to store contact information in address books, with keys representing names or contact IDs and values representing corresponding contact details.

14.1.2 Practice

Task: What are the real-life examples you can have for dictionaries?

14.2 CREATE A DICTIONARY

14.2.1 Demonstration

In Python, there are several methods for creating dictionaries, providing flexibility and convenience for different programming scenarios. Let's start with using the `dict()` constructor and key-value pairs:

```python
# Creating a dictionary using the dict() constructor and key-value pairs
my_dict = dict(name='Jane', age=25, city='Los Angeles')
print('Dictionary created using dict() constructor:', my_dict)
```

```
Dictionary created using dict() constructor:
{'name': 'Jane', 'age': 25, 'city': 'Los Angeles'}
```

```python
# Creating a dictionary using a list of tuples
my_list = [('name', 'Alice'), ('age', 35), ('city', 'Chicago')]
my_dict = dict(my_list)
print('Dictionary created using a list of tuples:', my_dict)
```

```
Dictionary created using a list of tuples:
{'name': 'Alice', 'age': 35, 'city': 'Chicago'}
```

Another approach to uing curly braces {} and key-value pairs:

```python
# Creating a dictionary using curly braces and key-value pairs
my_dict = {'name': 'John', 'age': 30, 'city': 'New York'}
print("Dictionary created using curly braces:", my_dict)
```

```
Dictionary created using curly braces:
{'name': 'John', 'age': 30, 'city': 'New York'}
```

```python
# Creating a dictionary using curly braces and key-value pairs
my_dict = {'name': ['John', 'Alice', 'Jane'],
           'age': [30, 35, 25],
           'city': ['New York', 'Chicago', 'Log Angeles']}
print("Dictionary created using curly braces:", my_dict)
```

```
Dictionary created using curly braces: {
'name': ['John', 'Alice', 'Jane'],
```

```
'age': [30, 35, 25],
'city': ['New York', 'Chicago', 'Log Angeles']}
```

In Python, the built-in function `len()` is used to determine the length or the number of key-value pairs in a dictionary.

```
print(my_dict)
print(len(my_dict)) # output 3
```

```
{'name': 'John', 'age': 30, 'city': 'New York'}
3
```

14.2.2 Practice

Task: Create a dictionary `weekdays` that contains key-value pairs that keys are the weekdays 1, ... , 7 and values are strings `'Monday'`, ..., `'Sunday'`. Print the dictionary together with its length.

```
weekdays = {1: 'Monday',
            2: 'Tuesday',
            3: 'Wednesday',
            4: 'Thursday',
            5: 'Friday',
            6: 'Saturday',
            7: 'Sunday'}
weekdays, len(weekdays)
```

```
({1: 'Monday',
  2: 'Tuesday',
  3: 'Wednesday',
  4: 'Thursday',
  5: 'Friday',
  6: 'Saturday',
  7: 'Sunday'},
 7)
```

Task: Create a dictionary `daysweek` that contains key-value pairs that keys are strings `'Monday'`, ..., `'Sunday'` and values are weekdays 1, ... , 7 and values. Print the dictionary together with its length.

```
daysweek = {'Monday': 1,
            'Tuesday': 2,
            'Wednesday': 3,
            'Thursday': 4,
            'Friday': 5,
            'Saturday': 6,
            'Sunday': 7}
daysweek, len(weekdays)
```

```
({'Monday': 1,
  'Tuesday': 2,
  'Wednesday': 3,
  'Thursday': 4,
  'Friday': 5,
  'Saturday': 6,
```

```
    'Sunday': 7},
  7)
```

Task: Create a dictionary `country_GDP` contains top 5 countries and their GDP 2023 estimate by World Bank. The keys are the names of the contry, and the values are their GDPs. The source is `https://en.wikipedia.org/wiki/List_of_countries_by_GDP_(nominal)`

```
country_GDP = {'United States': 25462700,
               'China': 17963171,
               'Germany': 4072192,
               'Japan': 4231141,
               'India': 3385090}
country_GDP
```

```
{'United States': 25462700,
 'China': 17963171,
 'Germany': 4072192,
 'Japan': 4231141,
 'India': 3385090}
```

Task: Create a dictionary `country_GDP_List` contains top 5 countries and their GDP 2023 estimate by World Bank. The keys `Name` has a list with the names of the contry and the key `GDP` has a list of their GDPs. The source is `https://en.wikipedia.org/wiki/List_of_countries_by_GDP_(nominal)`

```
country_GDP_List = {'Name': ['United States', 'China', 'Germany', 'Japan', 'India'],
                    'GDP': [25462700, 17963171, 4072192, 4231141, 3385090]}
country_GDP_List
```

```
{'Name': ['United States', 'China', 'Germany', 'Japan', 'India'],
 'GDP': [25462700, 17963171, 4072192, 4231141, 3385090]}
```

14.3 ACCESS A DICTIONARY

14.3.1 Demonstration

You can access the keys, values, or key-value pairs in a dictionary in Python.

You can access keys in a dictionary using the `keys()` method or directly iterate over the dictionary. The `keys()` method returns a view object containing the keys of the dictionary.

```
# Creating a dictionary
my_dict = {'name': 'John', 'age': 30, 'city': 'New York'}

# Accessing keys using keys() method
keys = my_dict.keys()
print('Keys:', keys)

# Accessing keys by iterating over the dictionary
for key in my_dict:
    print('Key:', key)
```

```
Keys: dict_keys(['name', 'age', 'city'])
Key: name
Key: age
Key: city
```

You can access values in a dictionary using the `values()` method or by directly accessing values using keys. The `values()` method returns a view object containing the values of the dictionary.

```
# Accessing values using values() method
values = my_dict.values()
print('Values:', values)

# Accessing values using keys
for key in my_dict:
    print(f'Value for key {key}: {my_dict[key]}')
```

```
Values: dict_values(['John', 30, 'New York'])
Value for key name: John
Value for key age: 30
Value for key city: New York
```

You can access items (key-value pairs) in a dictionary using the `items()` method or by directly iterating over the dictionary. The `items()` method returns a view object containing the key-value pairs of the dictionary as tuples.

```
# Accessing items using items() method
items = my_dict.items()
print('Items:', items)

# Accessing items by iterating over the dictionary
for key, value in my_dict.items():
    print(f'({key}: {value})')
```

```
Items: dict_items([('name', 'John'), ('age', 30), ('city', 'New York')])
(name: John)
(age: 30)
(city: New York)
```

14.3.2 Practice

Task: Iterate the dictionary **weekdays** and print each pair.

```
for item in weekdays.items():
  print(item)
```

```
(1, 'Monday')
(2, 'Tuesday')
(3, 'Wednesday')
(4, 'Thursday')
(5, 'Friday')
(6, 'Saturday')
(7, 'Sunday')
```

Task: Check the value associated with the key 1 in **weekdays**.

```
weekdays[1]
```

```
{"type":"string"}
```

Task: Iterate the dictionary `daysweek` and print each pair.

```
for item in daysweek.items():
  print(item)
```

```
('Monday', 1)
('Tuesday', 2)
('Wednesday', 3)
('Thursday', 4)
('Friday', 5)
('Saturday', 6)
('Sunday', 7)
```

Task: Check the value associated with the key `'Monday'` in `daysweek`.

```
daysweek['Monday']
```

```
1
```

Task: Iterate the dictionary `country_GDP` and print each pair.

```
for item in country_GDP.items():
  print(item)
```

```
('United States', 25452700)
('China', 17963171)
('Germany', 4072192)
('Japan', 4231141)
('India', 3385090)
```

Task: Check the value associated with the key `'United States'` in `country_GDP`.

```
country_GDP['United States']
```

```
25462700
```

Task: Print all countries that have GDP of more than $10 Trillion in `country_GDP`. Note: The unit in the table is Million.

```
for k, v in country_GDP.items():
  if v > 10000000:
    print(f'{k}:{v}')
```

```
United States:25462700
China:17963171
```

Task: Print the names of all countries in `country_GDP_List`.

```
country_GDP_List['Name']
```

```
['United States', 'China', 'Germany', 'Japan', 'India']
```

14.4   DICTIONARY METHODS

14.4.1   Demonstration

In Python, dictionaries offer various methods for manipulating key-value pairs, enabling efficient data management and modification. These methods facilitate the addition, deletion, and update of elements within dictionaries, ensuring flexibility and adaptability to changing data requirements.

To add a new `key:value` pair to a dictionary, we just need to use a `dict[key] = value` assignment.

```
# Creating a dictionary
my_dict = {'name': 'John', 'age': 30, 'city': 'New York'}

# Add a new pair 'ID': '0001'
my_dict['ID'] = '0001'

my_dict
```

```
{'name': 'John', 'age': 30, 'city': 'New York', 'ID': '0001'}
```

Be careful if there is an existing key in the dictionary. Doing a `dict[key] = value` assignment will use the new value to replace the old value associated with the key.

```
my_dict['name'] = 'Neo'

my_dict
```

```
{'name': 'Neo', 'age': 30, 'city': 'New York', 'ID': '0001'}
```

We can also use `update()` to add key-value pairs from another dictionary or iterable to the current dictionary.

```
# Creating another dictionary
another_dict = {'email':'John@example.com', 'major': 'English'}

my_dict.update(another_dict)

my_dict
```

```
{'name': 'Neo',
 'age': 30,
 'city': 'New York',
 'ID': '0001',
 'email': 'John@example.com',
 'major': 'English'}
```

```
# Creating a list of tuples
another_collection = [('phone', '123-456-7890'), ('fax', '098-765-4321')]

my_dict.update(another_collection)

my_dict
```

```
{'name': 'Neo',
 'age': 30,
 'city': 'New York',
 'ID': '0001',
 'email': 'John@example.com',
 'major': 'English',
 'phone': '123-456-7890',
 'fax': '098-765-4321'}
```

```
# Removing a key
del my_dict['fax']
my_dict
```

```
{'name': 'Neo',
 'age': 30,
 'city': 'New York',
 'ID': '0001',
 'email': 'John@example.com',
 'major': 'English',
 'phone': '123-456-7890'}
```

14.4.2 Practice

Task: Modify weekdays and make the strings with only one or two letters, such as 'M', 'Tu', 'W', 'Th', 'F', 'Sa', 'Su'.

```
weekdays[1] = 'M'
weekdays[2] = 'Tu'
weekdays[3] = 'W'
weekdays[4] = 'Th'
weekdays[5] = 'F'
weekdays[6] = 'Sa'
weekdays[7] = 'Su'
weekdays
```

```
{1: 'M', 2: 'Tu', 3: 'W', 4: 'Th', 5: 'F', 6: 'Sa', 7: 'Su'}
```

Task: Delete the keys 'Saturday', 'Sunday' in daysweek.

```
del daysweek['Saturday']
del daysweek['Sunday']
daysweek
```

```
{'Monday': 1, 'Tuesday': 2, 'Wednesday': 3, 'Thursday': 4, 'Friday': 5}
```

Task: Update country_GDP with the countries in #6-#10. The source is https://en.wikipedia.org/wiki/List_of_countries_by_GDP_(nominal).

```
more = {'United Kingdom': 3070668,
        'France': 2782905,
        'Brazil': 1920096,
        'Italy': 2010432,
        'Canada': 2139840}
country_GDP.update(more)
country_GDP
```

```
{'United States': 25462700,
 'China': 17963171,
 'Germany': 4072192,
 'Japan': 4231141,
 'India': 3385090,
 'United Kingdom': 3070668,
 'France': 2782905,
 'Brazil': 1920096,
 'Italy': 2010432,
 'Canada': 2139840}
```

Task: Add another key 'Population' to country_GDP_List. The value of this key is the population of the countries. The source is https://en.wikipedia.org/wiki/List_of_countries_and_dependencies_by_population.

```
country_GDP_List['Population'] = [335893238, 1409670000, 84607016,
        124000000, 1400744000]
country_GDP_List
```

```
{'name': ['United States', 'China', 'Germany', 'Japan', 'India'],
 'GDP': [25462700, 17963171, 4072192, 4231141, 3385090],
 'Population': [335893238, 1409670000, 84607016, 124000000, 1400744000]}
```

14.5   DICTIONARY COMPREHENSION

14.5.1   Demonstration

Dictionary comprehension, similar to list and set comprehensions, allows for the creation of dictionaries using a concise and efficient syntax in Python. Dictionary comprehension generates dictionaries by applying an expression to each item in an iterable, resulting in **key-value** pairs enclosed within curly braces {}.

The general syntax is:

```
dict_variable = {key expression: value expression for item in iterable condition}
```

```
# Using dictionary comprehension to generate a dictionary of squares
squares_dict = {x: x ** 2 for x in range(1, 6)}
print('Dictionary of squares:', squares_dict)
```

Dictionary of squares: {1: 1, 2: 4, 3: 9, 4: 16, 5: 25}

```
# Using dictionary comprehension to create a dictionary of word lengths
words = ['apple', 'banana', 'cherry']
word_lengths_dict = {word: len(word) for word in words}
print('Dictionary of word lengths:', word_lengths_dict)
```

Dictionary of word lengths: {'apple': 5, 'banana': 6, 'cherry': 6}

```
# Using dictionary comprehension to convert two lists into a dictionary
keys = ['a', 'b', 'c']
values = [1, 2, 3]
combined_dict = {keys[i]: values[i] for i in range(len(keys))}
print('Combined dictionary:', combined_dict)
```

Combined dictionary: {'a': 1, 'b': 2, 'c': 3}

```
# Create the double and square term for even numbers
even_degree = {x : [x*2, x**2] for x in range(10) if x %2 == 0}
print('Even numbers degrees:', even_degree)
```

Even numbers degrees: {0: [0, 0], 2: [4, 4], 4: [8, 16], 6: [12, 36], 8: [16, 64]}

14.5.2 Practice

Task: Ask user to enter a sentence, create a dictionary `word_length` mapping each word in a sentence to its length.

```
sentence = input('Please enter a sentence: ')

word_length = {word: len(word) for word in sentence.split()}
print('Dictionary mapping each word to its length:', word_length)
```

Please enter a sentence: Python is a useful language
Dictionary mapping each word to its length:
{'Python': 6, 'is': 2, 'a': 1, 'useful': 6, 'language': 8}

Task: Ask user to enter a sentence, create a dictionary `word_lengthy` mapping each word in a sentence to its length and ignore all words with length less than 3

```
sentence = input('Please enter a sentence: ')

word_lengthy = {word: len(word) for word in sentence.split() if len(word)>3}
print('Dictionary mapping each word to its length:', word_lengthy)
```

Please enter a sentence: Python is a useful language
Dictionary mapping each word to its length: {'Python': 6, 'useful': 6, 'language': 8}

Here, let's summarize what we learned about `set` in Table 14.1.

Table 14.1 Summary of Python dictionaries.

Feature	Syntax	Examples
Creation	`{}` or `dict()`	`my_dict = {"a": 1, "b": 2}`
		`my_dict = dict(a=1, b=2)`
Access	`dict[key]`	`my_dict["a"] → 1`
		Raises `KeyError` if the key does not exist.
Add	`dict[key] = value`	`my_dict["c"] = 3`
		`my_dict ⇒ {"a": 1, "b": 2, "c": 3}`
Remove	`dict.pop(key)`	`my_dict.pop("a")` returns 1
	`dict.popitem()`	`my_dict ⇒ {"b": 2}`
	`del dict[key]`	
Membership	`key in dict`	`"a" in my_dict → True.`
Elements	`dict.keys()`	`my_dict.keys() → dict_keys(["a", "b"])`
	`dict.values()`	`my_dict.values() → dict_values([1, 2])`
	`dict.items()`	`my_dict.items() → dict_items([("a", 1), ("b", 2)])`
Merging	`dict.update (other)`	`my_dict.update("c": 3)`
		`my_dict ⇒ {"a": 1, "b": 2, "c": 3}`

14.6 INTERACT WITH GENAI

Here are some questions and prompts you can interact with generative AI tools, including ChatGPT.

- Explain what a dictionary is in Python. How does it differ from other data structures like lists and sets?
- Discuss the concept of key-value pairs in dictionaries. Why is this structure useful for storing and accessing data?
- Describe common use cases for dictionaries, such as representing data with unique identifiers or mapping keys to corresponding values.
- Generate an example of creating a dictionary in Python with at least three key-value pairs. Demonstrate how to access a value using its key.
- Illustrate how to loop through a dictionary, accessing both keys and values using a `for` loop.
- Design an exercise for me to create a dictionary representing a contact list, with names as keys and phone numbers as values. Have them practice adding, updating, and deleting contacts.
- Create a task for me to write a Python function that takes a dictionary of student names and their grades and returns the name of the student with the highest grade.
- Develop an exercise for me to define a dictionary representing a shopping cart, with items as keys and quantities as values. Have them calculate the total number of items in the cart.

14.7 EXPLORE MORE OF DICTIONARY

In the end, here are the official documentations of Python `dict`:

- Brief introduction of dictionary: https://docs.python.org/3/library/stdtypes.html#mapping-types-dict
- More on dictionary: https://docs.python.org/3/tutorial/datastructures.html#dictionaries

## CHAPTER 15

Case Studies of Data Structures

W E have learned Python's four built-in data structures – lists, tuples, sets, and dictionaries! Let's apply them to a real-life scenario: managing and manipulating a grade book for students. In this case study, we will use each data structure to solve different problems, such as storing student information, organizing grades, ensuring uniqueness in data, and efficiently looking up specific records. By comparing and contrasting how each structure performs in this context, we can better understand their strengths and best use cases. Are you ready? Let's get started!

15.1 WARM-UP

Let's first warm-up what we have learned in this section in Table 15.1.

Table 15.1 Summary of Python data structures.

Feature	List	Tuple	Set	Dictionary
Constructor	`list()`	`tuple()`	`set()`	`dict()`
Access	Index, iteration	Index, iteration	Iteration only	Key, iteration
Slicing	Index	Index	Unordered	Unordered
Immutability	Mutable	Immutable	Mutable	Mutable
Methods	`append()`, `extend()`, `pop()`, `remove()`	`count()`, `index()`	`add()`, `remove()`, `pop()`	`get()`, `pop()`, `items()`, `keys()`, `values()`

DOI: 10.1201/9781003527725-15

15.2 DATA CREATION

You are given a dataset as below represented as a list. You should organize them in the required data structure in the following tasks.

```
# Run following cells for this case study
import random

SIZE = 10 # All upper case variable means it is a constant
names = ['STU' + str(i) for i in range(100,100+SIZE)]
scores1 = [random.randint(60, 100) for i in range(SIZE)]
scores2 = [random.randint(60, 100) for i in range(SIZE) ]
```

15.3 USING LISTS

Task: Create a grade book **gradebook** as a list, in which each element is a list and the first item is the name (from the **names** data), and second item is the score (from the **scores1** data).

```
gradebook = []
for i in range(len(names)):
    gradebook.append([names[i], scores1[i]])
gradebook
```

```
[['STU100', 85],
 ['STU101', 66],
 ['STU102', 89],
 ['STU103', 87],
 ['STU104', 100],
 ['STU105', 98],
 ['STU106', 86],
 ['STU107', 93],
 ['STU108', 74],
 ['STU109', 66]]
```

```
gradebook = [[name,score] for name,score in zip(names, scores1)]
gradebook
```

```
[['STU100', 85],
 ['STU101', 66],
 ['STU102', 89],
 ['STU103', 87],
 ['STU104', 100],
 ['STU105', 98],
 ['STU106', 86],
 ['STU107', 93],
 ['STU108', 74],
 ['STU109', 66]]
```

Task: Create a subset of the **gradebook** as **gb1**, which contains first 5 elements of the gradebook.

```
gb1 = gradebook[:5]
gb1
```

```
[['STU100', 85],
 ['STU101', 66],
 ['STU102', 89],
 ['STU103', 87],
 ['STU104', 100]]
```

Task: Create a subset of the **gradebook** as gb2, in which student name always ends with an even number.

```
gb2 = [v for v in gradebook if int(v[0][-1]) %2 == 0]
gb2
```

```
[['STU100', 85],
 ['STU102', 89],
 ['STU104', 100],
 ['STU106', 86],
 ['STU108', 74]]
```

Task: Create a subset of the **gradebook** as gb3, in which student score always above 80.

```
gb3 = [v for v in gradebook if v[1] > 80]
gb3
```

```
[['STU100', 85],
 ['STU102', 89],
 ['STU103', 87],
 ['STU104', 100],
 ['STU105', 98],
 ['STU106', 86],
 ['STU107', 93]]
```

Task: Create a subset of the **gradebook** as gb4, in which student scores are below the average score.

```
total = 0
for s in scores1:
  total += s
avg = total / len(scores1)
gb4 = [v for v in gradebook if v[1] < avg]
gb4
```

```
[['STU101', 66], ['STU108', 74], ['STU109', 66]]
```

Task: Update the **gradebook** so the scores are converted to letter grade: >=90 is A, >=80 is B, etc.

```
def g21(score):
    letters = ['F','F','F','F','F','F','D','C','B','A','A']
    return letters[score//10]

gradebook = [[v[0],g21(v[1])] for v in gradebook]
gradebook
```

```
[['STU100', 'B'],
 ['STU101', 'D'],
 ['STU102', 'B'],
 ['STU103', 'B'],
 ['STU104', 'A'],
 ['STU105', 'A'],
 ['STU106', 'B'],
 ['STU107', 'A'],
 ['STU108', 'C'],
 ['STU109', 'D']]
```

15.4 USING TUPLES

Task: Create a `gradebook` as a list, in which each element is a tuple and the first item is the name (from the `names` data), and second item is the score (from the `scores1` data).

```
gradebook = [(name,score) for name,score in zip(names, scores1)]
gradebook
```

```
[('STU100', 85),
 ('STU101', 66),
 ('STU102', 89),
 ('STU103', 87),
 ('STU104', 100),
 ('STU105', 98),
 ('STU106', 86),
 ('STU107', 93),
 ('STU108', 74),
 ('STU109', 66)]
```

Task: Traverse the `gradebook` and print out student name ends with an even number.

```
gb2 = [v for v in gradebook if int(v[0][-1]) %2 == 0]
gb2
```

```
[('STU100', 85),
 ('STU102', 89),
 ('STU104', 100),
 ('STU106', 86),
 ('STU108', 74)]
```

Task: Update the `gradebook` so the scores are converted to letter grade: >=90 is A, >=80 is B, etc.

```
def g21(score):
    letters = ['F','F','F','F','F','F','D','C','B','A', 'A']
    return letters[score//10]

gradebook = [(v[0],g21(v[1])) for v in gradebook]
gradebook
```

```
[('STU100', 'B'),
 ('STU101', 'D'),
```

```
('STU102', 'B'),
('STU103', 'B'),
('STU104', 'A'),
('STU105', 'A'),
('STU106', 'B'),
('STU107', 'A'),
('STU108', 'C'),
('STU109', 'D')]
```

15.5   USING SETS

Task: We have `scores1` and `scores2`. Convert them to `set1` and `set2`.

```
set1 = set(scores1)
set1
```

{66, 74, 85, 86, 87, 89, 93, 98, 100}

```
set2 = set(scores2)
set2
```

{60, 64, 67, 72, 73, 75, 91, 92, 97}

Task: Print the unique score in `scores1` and unique score in `scores2` .

```
print(set1, set2)
```

{66, 98, 100, 74, 85, 86, 87, 89, 93} {64, 97, 67, 72, 73, 75, 92, 91, 60}

Task: Print the union of `set1` and `set2`.

```
print(set1.union(set2)) # same as set1 | set2
```

{64, 97, 66, 98, 100, 67, 72, 73, 74, 75, 60, 85, 86, 87, 89, 91, 92, 93}

Task: Print the intersection of `set1` and `set2`.

```
print(set1.intersection(set2)) # same as set1 & set2
```

set()

Task: Print the difference of `set1` and `set2`.

```
print(set1.difference(set2)) # same as set1 - set2
```

{66, 98, 100, 74, 85, 86, 87, 89, 93}

15.6   USING DICTIONARIES

Task: Create a dictionary `d1`, in which names as key and `scores1` as values.

```
d1 = {name:score1 for name, score1 in zip(names, scores1)}
d1
```

```
{'STU100': 85,
 'STU101': 66,
 'STU102': 89,
 'STU103': 87,
 'STU104': 100,
 'STU105': 98,
 'STU106': 86,
 'STU107': 93,
 'STU108': 74,
 'STU109': 66}
```

Task: Print the score of the student with name `'STU103'`.

```
print(d1['STU103'])
```

87

Task: Create a dictionary d2, in which names as key and `scores2` as values.

```
d2 = {name:score2 for name, score2 in zip(names, scores2)}
d2
```

```
{'STU100': 75,
 'STU101': 60,
 'STU102': 72,
 'STU103': 92,
 'STU104': 97,
 'STU105': 64,
 'STU106': 73,
 'STU107': 67,
 'STU108': 91,
 'STU109': 97}
```

Task: Print the names of student whose score is 88.

```
for name in d2:
    if d2[name] == 88:
        print(name)
```

Task: Create a dictionary d3, in which names as key, and a list of scores as value. The list of scores has two elements: the first one is from `scores1` , and the second one is from `scores2` .

```
d3 = {name:[score1, score2]
      for name, score1, score2 in zip(names, scores1, scores2)}
d3
```

```
{'STU100': [85, 75],
 'STU101': [66, 60],
 'STU102': [89, 72],
 'STU103': [87, 92],
 'STU104': [100, 97],
 'STU105': [98, 64],
 'STU106': [86, 73],
 'STU107': [93, 67],
 'STU108': [74, 91],
```

```
'STU109': [66, 97]}
```

Task: Find the cluster of students whose scores are all at least 90.

```
students_A = {s:[d3[s][0], d3[s][1]]
              for s in d3
              if d3[s][0] >=90 and d3[s][1] >=90}
students_A
```

```
{'STU104': [100, 97]}
```

15.7 FURTHERMORE

Task: Did you notice the constant variable SIZE we used in data creation? Now, you can change that variable to 100, 1000, 10000, or even more, to observe the differences of the data structures in efficiency when we scale the data up. Enjoy the exploration!

15.8 COMPLEXITY

We select a data structure for a specific scenario based on its time and space complexity, which represents how efficiently the data structure performs in scaling. For those interested in complexity theory, a concise summary of the complexity of typical operations on data structures is presented in Table 15.2. While we will not cover complexity in detail in this book, there are many excellent resources available online for further exploration. Enjoy the learning!

Table 15.2 Comparison of space and time complexities for Python data structures. (list, tuple, set, dictionary)

Operation	List	Tuple	Set	Dictionary
Space	O(n)	O(n)	O(n)	O(n)
Add	O(1) (append)	Not applicable	O(1)	O(1)
Remove	O(n)(by value) O(1)(by index)	Not applicable	O(1)	O(1)
Insert	O(n)(at index)	Not applicable	Not applicable	O(1)
Search	O(n)	O(n)	O(1)	O(1)
Iteration	O(n)	O(n)	O(n)	O(n)
Membership	O(n)	O(n)	O(1)	O(1)
Concatenate	O(n)	O(n)	Not applicable	O(n)
Copy	O(n) (shallow)	O(n) (shallow)	O(n) (shallow)	O(n) (shallow)
Equality	O(n)	O(n)	O(n)	O(n)

IV

Data Collections

S ECTION IV: DATA COLLECTIONS introduces Python's `collections` module, which offers advanced data structures that extend beyond basic types, making data manipulation easier and more efficient. In this section, we'll explore three essential tools from the `collections` module: `namedtuple`, which gives tuples meaningful names; `defaultdict`, which simplifies handling missing keys; and `Counter`, which makes counting tasks effortless. These structures enhance code readability and functionality, helping you solve problems more effectively.

By the end of this chapter, you will be able to:

- Understand the purpose and benefits of the `collections` module in Python.

- Create and use named tuples to add clarity and structure to your data.

- Implement default dictionaries to handle missing keys without errors.

- Use counters to efficiently count and analyze data elements.

- Apply these data structures in practical scenarios to simplify and optimize your code.

## CHAPTER 16

Named Tuple

W E have learned `tuple` in previous section and we know `tuple` is useful for grouping related data, but its elements are accessed only by position, which can make the code less readable and harder to maintain. In this chapter, we are going to learn the extended data structure, `namedtuple`, which addresses this limitation by allowing you to assign meaningful names to each element while retaining the immutability and lightweight nature of regular tuples. This makes `namedtuple` especially helpful for improving code clarity and reducing the risk of errors in larger projects where readability is critical. Are you ready? Let's get started!

16.1 WHAT IS A NAMED TUPLE

16.1.1 Explanation

Named Tuples are an extension of Python's built-in `tuple` data type. They allow for creating tuple-like objects where fields can be accessed using names, instead of only by index. This can make code more readable and easier to maintain, especially when dealing with collections of data that have multiple attributes.

Named Tuples are part of the `collections` module in Python, and they're typically used to represent simple data structures without the overhead of a full class. They're a great tool when you want the simplicity of tuples but with named fields to provide clarity.

16.1.2 Demonstration

Let's create a tuple to represent the position of a data point in a 2D space with x and y coordinates.

```python
# Regular tuple example
position1_tuple = (10, 20)
position2_tuple = (-5, 30)

# Accessing data using index
```

DOI: 10.1201/9781003527725-16

```
print(f'Position 1: x={position1_tuple[0]}, y={position1_tuple[1]}')
print(f'Position 2: x={position2_tuple[0]}, y={position2_tuple[1]}')
```

```
Position 1: x=10, y=20
Position 2: x=-5, y=30
```

In the regular tuple, you need to use the index 0 for x and 1 for y, which isn't as intuitive and may lead to confusion in larger programs.

Let's create a named tuple to represent the data point.

```
from collections import namedtuple

# Define the named tuple 'Position'
Position = namedtuple('Position', ['x', 'y'])

# Creating instances of the named tuple
position1 = Position(x=10, y=20)
position2 = Position(x=-5, y=30)

# Accessing data using named fields
print(f"Position 1: x={position1.x}, y={position1.y}")
print(f"Position 2: x={position2.x}, y={position2.y}")
```

```
Position 1: x=10, y=20
Position 2: x=-5, y=30
```

With the named tuple Position, you can access x and y using descriptive names (position1.x, position1.y), making the code more readable and self-explanatory.

16.2 PACKAGE MANAGEMENT

Let's imagine a scenario where you work in a logistics company, and you manage packages being delivered. Each package has attributes like sender, receiver, and status. Using Named Tuples, we can clearly label each attribute, making it easy to access information about any package.

```
from collections import namedtuple

# Defining the named tuple 'Package'
Package = namedtuple('Package', ['sender', 'receiver', 'status'])

# Creating instances of the named tuple
package1 = Package(sender="Alice", receiver="Bob", status="Delivered")
package2 = Package(sender="Eve", receiver="Chris", status="In Transit")

# Accessing data by field names
print(f'Package1 sender: {package1.sender}, status: {package1.status}')
print(f'Package2 receiver: {package2.receiver}, status: {package2.status}')

# Accessing data by index (just like a normal tuple)
print(f'Package1: {package1[0]} to {package1[1]}, status: {package1[2]}')
print(f'Package2: {package2[0]} to {package2[1]}, status: {package2[2]}')
```

```
Package1 sender: Alice, status: Delivered
Package2 receiver: Chris, status: In Transit
Package1: Alice to Bob, status: Delivered
Package2: Eve to Chris, status: In Transit
```

In this example, `Package` is a named tuple with fields `sender`, `receiver`, and `status`. `package1` and `package2` are instances of `Package`. You can access fields either by their name (like `package1.sender`) or by their index (like `package1[0]`).

16.3   CASE STUDY: CAR

Task: Define a named tuple to represent a `Car` with the fields: `make`, `model`, `year`, and `color`. Create two instances of this named tuple and print out the details of each car.

```python
from collections import namedtuple

# Define the Car namedtuple
Car = namedtuple('Car', ['make', 'model', 'year', 'color'])

# Create instances of Car
car1 = Car(make="Toyota", model="Corolla", year=2020, color="Blue")
car2 = Car(make="Honda", model="Civic", year=2019, color="Red")

# Print car details
print(f'Car 1: {car1.make} {car1.model}, {car1.year}, {car1.color}')
print(f'Car 2: {car2.make} {car2.model}, {car2.year}, {car2.color}')
```

```
Car 1: Toyota Corolla, 2020, Blue
Car 2: Honda Civic, 2019, Red
```

16.4   INTERACT WITH GENAI

Here are some questions and prompts you can interact with generative AI tools, including ChatGPT about `namedtuples`:

- Why should I use `namedtuple` instead of a dictionary or regular tuple?
- What are the advantages and limitations of using `namedtuple`?
- What happens if I try to access a field in a `namedtuple` that doesn't exist?
- Can I add new fields to an existing `namedtuple`? Why or why not?
- How does a `namedtuple` behave when compared using equality operators?
- How do I use _replace() to create a modified copy of a `namedtuple`?
- Can you explain the purpose of _fields and _asdict() in a `namedtuple`?
- Show how to create a `namedtuple` with default field values.
- Demonstrate how to unpack a `namedtuple` using tuple unpacking.
- How can I use `namedtuple` in a data analysis pipeline?
- Why am I getting an error when I try to modify a field in my `namedtuple`?
- What does it mean if I see an AttributeError in my `namedtuple`?
- What are common mistakes people make when using `namedtuple`?

16.5 EXPLORE MORE OF NAMED TUPLE

At the end, here are the official documentations of Python `namedtuple`:

- Brief introduction of named tuple: https://docs.python.org/3/library/collections.html#collections.namedtuple

## CHAPTER 17

Default Dictionary

D ICTIONARIES are excellent for storing key-value pairs, but accessing a key that doesn't exist raises a KeyError. Default dictionaries build on this functionality by automatically assigning a default value to missing keys, eliminating the need for manual checks or initialization. This makes default dictionaries especially useful when working with dynamic or unpredictable data where keys might not always exist in advance. In this chapter, we will explore defaultdict from the collections module in Python. We first demonstrate the difference between a regular dictionary dict and a default dictionary defaultdict, then explore different types of defaultdict, including int, list, and set.

Are you ready? Let's get started!

17.1 WHAT IS A DEFAULT DICTIONARY

When we use a key to retrieve the value, and the key is not in the dictionary, the regular dictionary dict will raise an error.

```python
# Regular dictionary
my_dict = {'a': 1, 'b': 2}

# Accessing an existing key
print(my_dict['a'])  # Output: 1

# Accessing a non-existing key will raise a KeyError
print(my_dict['c'])  # KeyError: 'c'
```

1

```
-------------------------------------------------------------------
KeyError                            Traceback (most recent call last)
<ipython-input-2-2e2cefa552f4> in <cell line: 8>()
      6
      7 # Accessing a non-existing key will raise a KeyError
----> 8 print(my_dict['c'])  # KeyError: 'c'
```

DOI: 10.1201/9781003527725-17

```
KeyError: 'c'
```

When we want to modify the value associated with a key, and the key is not in the dictionary, the regular dictionary dict will raise an error.

```
# Increament the value associated with 'b' by 1
my_dict['b'] += 1
print(my_dict['b'])

# Increament the value associated with 'd' by 1
my_dict['d'] += 1
print(my_dict['d'])
```

5

```
---------------------------------------------------------------------
KeyError                              Traceback (most recent call last)
<ipython-input-5-4d2dcf7f0151> in <cell line: 6>()
      4
      5 # Increament the value associated with 'd' by 1
----> 6 my_dict['d'] += 1
      7 print(my_dict['d'])

KeyError: 'd'
```

In order to avoid this, we have to first check if the key is in the dictionary or not.

```
# Accessing values after checking keys
keys = ['a', 'c']
for key in keys:
  if key in my_dict:
    print(my_dict[key])
  else:
    print(f'{key} is not in the dictionary')
```

```
1
c is not in the dictionary
```

```
# Manipulate the values after checking keys
keys = ['b', 'd']
for key in keys:
  if key in my_dict:
    my_dict[key] += 1
  else:
    my_dict[key] = 1
print(my_dict)
```

```
{'a': 1, 'b': 3, 'd': 1}
```

A defaultdict simplifies handling missing keys by automatically assigning a default value when a non-existing key is accessed. You don't have to check if the key exists; instead, the default value is returned and assigned automatically.

```
from collections import defaultdict

# defaultdict with default type int (0 as default value for missing keys)
```

```
my_defaultdict = defaultdict(int)
my_defaultdict['a'] = 1
my_defaultdict['b'] = 2

print(my_defaultdict['a'])  # Output: 1
print(my_defaultdict['c'])  # Output: 0 (default value)
```

```
1
0
```

```
my_defaultdict['b'] += 1
print(my_defaultdict['b']) # output: 3 (existing value 2 increased by 1)

my_defaultdict['d'] += 1
print(my_defaultdict['d']) # output: 1 (default value)
```

```
3
1
```

Key difference between `dict` and `defaultdict` are `dict` raises an error when a missing key is accessed, while `defaultdict` returns a default value and avoids the need for manual checking.

17.2 DEFAULT INT

17.2.1 Demonstration

Like the example we had above, when you want to have values as numbers, such as in a situation where you need to count occurrences of items (e.g., counting words in a text), `defaultdict(int)` is useful since it initializes missing keys with a default integer value (0).

```
from collections import defaultdict

# Define the defaultdict with int 0 as the default value
word_count = defaultdict(int)

# Example text
text = 'hello world python world'

# Count word occurrences
for word in text.split():
    word_count[word] += 1

# Display word frequencies
print(word_count)
```

```
defaultdict(<class 'int'>, {'hello': 1, 'world': 2, 'python': 1})
```

17.2.2 Practice

Task: Use a `defaultdict` to count the number of orders placed by customers in an online store. Simulate several orders for different customers as:

```
Alice: 1 order;
Bob: 2 orders;
Charlie: 3 orders;
Alice: 1 order;
Charlie: 1 order.
```

Print the total order count for each customer.

```python
from collections import defaultdict

# Create a defaultdict with int 0 as the default value
order_count = defaultdict(int)

# Simulating order placement
order_count['Alice'] += 1
order_count['Bob'] += 2
order_count['Charlie'] += 3
order_count['Alice'] += 1
order_count['Charlie'] += 1

# Display the total order count for each customer
print('Total orders placed by each customer:')
for customer, count in order_count.items():
    print(f'{customer}: {count} orders')
```

```
Total orders placed by each customer:
Alice: 2 orders
Bob: 2 orders
Charlie: 4 orders
```

17.3   DEFAULT LIST

17.3.1   Demonstration

If you need to collect multiple values for a single key (e.g., students enrolled in the same course), `defaultdict(list)` is helpful because it initializes missing keys with an empty list.

```python
from collections import defaultdict

# Define defaultdict with an empty list as the default value
students_by_course = defaultdict(list)

# Add students to courses
students_by_course['CS'].append('Alice')
students_by_course['CS'].append('Bob')
students_by_course['Stats'].append('Charlie')

# Display students grouped by course
print(students_by_course)
```

```
defaultdict(<class 'list'>, {'CS': ['Alice', 'Bob'], 'Stats': ['Charlie']})
```

17.3.2   Practice

Task: Group people based on their city. Add several people and their cities as:

```
Alice: New York
Bob: New York
Charlie: Los Angeles
Dave: Chicago
Eve: Los Angeles
```

Print the grouped results based on their city.

```python
from collections import defaultdict

# Create a defaultdict with an empty list as the default value
people_by_city = defaultdict(list)

# Adding people and their respective cities
people_by_city['New York'].append('Alice')
people_by_city['New York'].append('Bob')
people_by_city['Los Angeles'].append('Charlie')
people_by_city['Chicago'].append('Dave')
people_by_city['Los Angeles'].append('Eve')

# Display the grouped result
print('People grouped by city:')
for city, people in people_by_city.items():
    print(f'{city}: {", ".join(people)}')
```

```
People grouped by city:
New York: Alice, Bob
Los Angeles: Charlie, Eve
Chicago: Dave
```

17.4   DEFAULT SET

17.4.1   Demonstration

In cases where you want to store unique values for each key (e.g., tracking unique visitors per webpage), `defaultdict(set)` automatically provides an empty set for missing keys.

```python
from collections import defaultdict

# Define defaultdict with an empty set as the default value
unique_visitors = defaultdict(set)

# Log unique visitors
unique_visitors['homepage'].add('User1')
unique_visitors['homepage'].add('User2')
unique_visitors['contact'].add('User1')
unique_visitors['homepage'].add('User1')  # User1 won't be added again
```

```
# Display unique visitors
print(unique_visitors)
```

```
defaultdict(<class 'set'>, {'homepage': {'User2', 'User1'}, 'contact': {'User1'}})
```

17.4.2   Practice

Task: A company wants to keep track of the skills that each department's employees have. Employees may have multiple skills, and each skill should be grouped under the department they belong to. Create a `defaultdict` that groups employees' skills by department and then display the result. Employees and their skills:

- HR: Alice (Communication, Management), Ann (Recruitment, Management)
- IT: Bob (Python, Networking), Charlie (Python)
- Sales: Eve (Negotiation, Communication), Davis (Communication, Networking)

```
from collections import defaultdict

# Define defaultdict with an empty set as the default value
department_skills = defaultdict(set)

# Simulating the addition of employees and their skills by department
department_skills['HR'].add('Communication')
department_skills['HR'].add('Management')
department_skills['HR'].add('Recruitment')
department_skills['HR'].add('Management') # Duplicates
department_skills['IT'].add('Python')
department_skills['IT'].add('Networking')
department_skills['IT'].add('Python')   # Duplicates
department_skills['Sales'].add('Negotiation')
department_skills['Sales'].add('Communication')
department_skills['Sales'].add('Communication') # Duplicates
department_skills['Sales'].add('Networking')

# Display the skills grouped by department
print('Skills grouped by department:')
for department, skills in department_skills.items():
    print(f'{department}: {", ".join(skills)}')
```

```
Skills grouped by department:
HR: Recruitment, Communication, Management
IT: Networking, Python
Sales: Negotiation, Communication, Networking
```

17.5   CASE STUDY: HACKATHON

Task: You are organizing a hackathon and need to manage participants, their projects, and the prizes they win. Use a `defaultdict` to collect and display:

1. Participants by team (using `list`).
2. Total prize money won by each team (using `int`).

Problem Setup:

- There are three teams: "Team A", "Team B", and "Team C".
- Participants are as follows:
  - Team A: Alice, Bob
  - Team B: Charlie, Dave
  - Team C: Eve, Frank
- Prizes won:
  - Team A: $500
  - Team B: $300
  - Team C: $1000

Create a Python program to:

1. Display the participants in each team.
2. Calculate and display the total prize money for each team.

```python
from collections import defaultdict

# 1. Participants by team (defaultdict with list)
teams = defaultdict(list)
teams['Team A'].extend(['Alice', 'Bob'])
teams['Team B'].extend(['Charlie', 'Dave'])
teams['Team C'].extend(['Eve', 'Frank'])

# 2. Total prize money by team (defaultdict with int)
prizes = defaultdict(int)
prizes['Team A'] += 500
prizes['Team B'] += 300
prizes['Team C'] += 1000

# Display team participants
print('Participants by team:')
for team, members in teams.items():
    print(f'{team}: {", ".join(members)}')

# Display total prize money won by each team
print('\nTotal prize money by team:')
for team, prize in prizes.items():
    print(f'{team}: ${prize}')
```

```
Participants by team:
Team A: Alice, Bob
Team B: Charlie, Dave
Team C: Eve, Frank

Total prize money by team:
Team A: $500
Team B: $300
Team C: $1000
```

Let's summarize the default dictionary in Table 17.1.

Table 17.1 Summary of Python defaultdict with different default values.

Feature	list as default	int as default	str as default	set as default
Creation	defaultdict (list)	defaultdict (int)	defaultdict (str)	defaultdict (set)
Default Value	[]	0	" "	{}
Default Behavior	Initializes an empty list if a non-existing key is accessed	Initializes to 0 if a non-existing key is accessed	Initializes to an empty string if a non-existing key is accessed	Initializes to an empty set if a non-existing key is accessed
New Key	my_dict["a"] returns []	my_dict["a"] returns 0	my_dict["a"] returns ""	my_dict["a"] returns {}
Usage	my_dict["a"] .append(1) adds 1 to the list	my_dict["a"] += 1 increments the value by 1	my_dict["a"] += "Hi" appends "Hi" to the string	my_dict["a"] .add(1) adds 1 to the set

17.6 INTERACT WITH GENAI

Here are some questions and prompts you can interact with generative AI tools, including ChatGPT about defaultdict:

- What is a defaultdict, and how is it different from a regular dictionary?
- Can you explain how missing keys are handled in a defaultdict?
- What are the limitations or drawbacks of using a defaultdict?
- Create a defaultdict to count the occurrences of elements in a list.
- Create a defaultdict to group words by the first letter from a list of strings.
- If I try to access a missing key in a defaultdict, what happens?
- What happens if I assign a value to a key that is already in the defaultdict?
- How can a defaultdict be used to process and summarize log files?
- Show how a defaultdict can implement a word frequency counter.
- Suggest a way to use defaultdict in data aggregation.
- Why do I get unexpected values when I print my defaultdict?
- How do I handle cases where I don't want any default value for missing keys in a defaultdict?
- What are common mistakes when using defaultdict?

17.7 EXPLORE MORE OF DEFAULT DICTIONARY

At the end, here are the official documentations of Python defaultdict:

- Brief introduction of default dictionary: https://docs.python.org/3/library/coll ections.html#collections.defaultdict

## CHAPTER 18

Counters

D ICTIONARIES store key-value pairs efficiently, but managing missing keys can be cumbersome. Default dictionaries improve this by assigning default values to missing keys automatically. Taking this further, the Counter is a specialized type of dictionary designed specifically for counting tasks. While default dictionaries simplify handling missing keys, Counters streamline tasks like counting elements, making them perfect for frequency analysis and similar operations. In this chapter, we will explore the `Counter` from Python's `collections` module. We will start by comparing it with a normal dictionary and `defaultdict`, then introduce the `Counter` in detail, followed by real-life demonstrations and practice problems with solutions.

Are you ready? Let's get started!

18.1   WHAT IS A COUNTER

Let's do a fruit count exercise first using normal dictionary.

```python
# Using a normal dictionary to count occurrences
fruit_count = {}
basket = ['apple', 'banana', 'apple', 'orange', 'banana', 'banana']

for fruit in basket:
    if fruit in fruit_count:
        fruit_count[fruit] += 1
    else:
        fruit_count[fruit] = 1

print(fruit_count)
```

```
{'apple': 2, 'banana': 3, 'orange': 1}
```

We definitely can use `defaultdict(int)` to save some effort.

```python
from collections import defaultdict

# Using defaultdict to count occurrences
```

DOI: 10.1201/9781003527725-18

```
fruit_count = defaultdict(int)
basket = ['apple', 'banana', 'apple', 'orange', 'banana', 'banana']

for fruit in basket:
    fruit_count[fruit] += 1

print(fruit_count)
```

```
defaultdict(<class 'int'>, {'apple': 2, 'banana': 3, 'orange': 1})
```

Counter goes one step further by providing an easy-to-use tool for counting elements in an iterable. It automatically counts the occurrences of elements without needing a loop, making the code cleaner and faster to write.

```
from collections import Counter

# Using Counter to count occurrences
basket = ['apple', 'banana', 'apple', 'orange', 'banana', 'banana']
fruit_count = Counter(basket)

print(fruit_count)
```

```
Counter({'banana': 3, 'apple': 2, 'orange': 1})
```

18.2   MORE ABOUT COUNTER

18.2.1   Explanation

The Counter class is a subclass of dict designed to count hashable objects. It automatically counts how many times an element appears in an iterable. You can create a Counter directly from an iterable or manually from a dictionary. The counts are stored as dictionary values, with elements as keys. Counter.most_common() returns a sorted list of the most frequent elements.

18.2.2   Demonstration

A store sells fruits, and we want to know how many of each type have been sold at the end of the day.

```
from collections import Counter

# Record of items sold
items_sold = ['apple', 'banana', 'apple', 'orange', 'apple',
              'banana', 'banana', 'orange', 'apple']

# Use Counter to count the sold items
item_count = Counter(items_sold)

# Display the count of each item
print('Items sold count:', item_count)

# Find the most sold item
most_sold = item_count.most_common(1)
```

```
print('Most sold item:', most_sold)

# Find the top 2 sold item
top2_sold = item_count.most_common(2)
print('Top 2 sold item:', top2_sold)
```

```
Items sold count: Counter({'apple': 4, 'banana': 3, 'orange': 2})
Most sold item: [('apple', 4)]
Top 2 sold item: [('apple', 4), ('banana', 3)]
```

We want to count how many times each letter appears in a given sentence.

```
from collections import Counter

sentence = "Python is a powerful programming language"

# Use Counter to count letter frequencies
letter_count = Counter(sentence.replace(' ', '').lower())

print("Top 5 letter count:", letter_count.most_common(5))
```

```
Top 5 letter count: [('a', 4), ('g', 4), ('p', 3), ('o', 3), ('n', 3)]
```

18.2.3 Practice

Task: Given a list of words from a book or paragraph as below:

```
paragraph = '''
Python is a high-level, general-purpose programming language. Its design
philosophy emphasizes code readability with the use of indentation.

Python is dynamically typed and garbage-collected. It supports multiple
programming paradigms, including structured (particularly procedural),
object-oriented and functional programming. It is often described as a
"batteries included" language due to its comprehensive standard library.

Guido van Rossum began working on Python in the late 1980s as a successor
to the ABC programming language and first released it in 1991 as
Python 0.9.0. Python 2.0 was released in 2000. Python 3.0, released in 2008,
was a major revision not completely backward-compatible with earlier
versions. Python 2.7.18, released in 2020, was the last release of Python 2.

Python consistently ranks as one of the most popular programming languages,
and has gained widespread use in the machine learning community.
'''
```

count how many times each word appears (ignore cases). Print the top 10 most used words with their frequency.

```
from collections import Counter
# Define the paragraph
paragraph = '''
Python is a high-level, general-purpose programming language. Its design
philosophy emphasizes code readability with the use of indentation.

Python is dynamically typed and garbage-collected. It supports multiple
```

```
programming paradigms, including structured (particularly procedural),
object-oriented and functional programming. It is often described as a
"batteries included" language due to its comprehensive standard library.

Guido van Rossum began working on Python in the late 1980s as a successor
to the ABC programming language and first released it in 1991 as Python
0.9.0. Python 2.0 was released in 2000. Python 3.0, released in  2008, was
a major revision not completely backward-compatible with earlier versions.
Python 2.7.18, released in 2020, was the last release of Python 2.

Python consistently ranks as one of the most popular programming
languages, and has gained widespread use in the machine learning community.
'''

# Use Counter to count word frequencies
word_count = Counter(paragraph.lower().split())

for word, count in word_count.most_common(10):
    print(f'{word}: {count}')
```

```
python: 9
the: 6
in: 6
a: 4
programming: 4
and: 4
as: 4
released: 4
is: 3
of: 3
```

Task: Given a list of numbers as below:

```
numbers = [1, 3, 2, 2, 3, 3, 4, 5, 1, 2, 2, 4, 1]
```

Find and print the top 3 most frequent numbers.

```
from collections import Counter

# List of numbers
numbers = [1, 3, 2, 2, 3, 3, 4, 5, 1, 2, 2, 4, 1]

# Use Counter to find the most common numbers
number_count = Counter(numbers)

# Display the top 3 most common numbers
print("Top 3 most common numbers:", number_count.most_common(3))
```

```
Top 3 most common numbers: [(2, 4), (1, 3), (3, 3)]
```

18.3   CASE STUDY: ROMEO AND JULIET

Task: In this exercise, you will create a counter that holds the most common words used and the number of times they show up in the masterpiece of Shakespeare, Romeo and Juliet. You need to find a text file that contains the full play, then feed it to a list with appropriate manipulation. After that, use Counter to quickly summarize the frequency of words in it.

For example, you may find it via https://shakespeare.mit.edu/romeo_juliet/full.html

To save space, solution for this case study is not provided.

18.4 INTERACT WITH GENAI

Here are some questions and prompts you can interact with generative AI tools, including ChatGPT about `Counter`:

- What is a `Counter` in Python, and how is it different from a dictionary?
- How does `Counter` count elements in an iterable?
- What are the primary use cases for `Counter` in Python?
- Show how to use `Counter` to count the frequency of elements in a list.
- Show how to create a `Counter` from a string to count character occurrences.
- Show how to update a `Counter` with additional data from another iterable.
- What happens if I access a key in a `Counter` that doesn't exist?
- How does the `most_common()` method in `Counter` work?
- How does a `Counter` handle duplicate keys during initialization?
- How can I use `Counter` to merge counts from multiple data sources?
- Show how to use `Counter` to filter elements based on a count threshold.
- How can I use mathematical operations like addition or subtraction between two `Counter` objects?
- How might `Counter` be applied in a social media app to track hashtags?
- Demonstrate using `Counter` to analyze survey results, such as the most selected options.
- How can `Counter` simplify tasks like vote tallying in an election system?
- Why am I getting a `TypeError` when I try to use a list as a key in a `Counter`?
- What happens if I attempt to increment a `Counter` key by a non-integer value?
- How do I handle negative counts in a `Counter` when they don't make sense in my context?

18.5 EXPLORE MORE OF COUNTER

At the end, here are the official documentations of Python `Counter`:

- Brief introduction of counters: https://docs.python.org/3/library/collections.html#collections.Counter

What is Next?

Congratulations! You have mastered basic Python with a full understanding of the fundamental syntax, flow control, functions, and built-in data structures. You are not a beginner anymore, and you can create your own Python programs to solve some real-life problems! Is that cool?

After the celebration, you may want to learn how the built-in data types and data structures are defined following the object-oriented programming logic. You may want to explore advanced data structures to store data differently for specific scenarios. You may also be interested in widely used Python packages for data manipulation, including Random, Math, NumPy, and Pandas. At last, for a better understanding of the data and communication of the statistics, you may want to learn data visualization packages, such as Matplotlib, Seaborn, and Plotly. You can find these topics covered in the second book of the series, *BiteSize Python for Intermediate Learners: With Practice Labs, Real World Examples, and ChatGPT*.

I look forward to meeting you there and continuing our journey once again.

Index

Anaconda, 8
Argument, 89
Arithmetic operations, 26, 27
Assignment operations, 26

Bite-size strategy, 8
bool, 19
break, 78

collections, 190
Complexity, 187
continue, 78
Counter, 190, 203

Data collections, 190
Data structure, 118, 119
Data type, 19
Data visualization, 6
Default dictionary, 190, 195
Default value, 96
defaultdict, 190, 195
Dictionary, 170
Dynamic typing, 21

Experiential learning, 8

f-strings, 43
float, 19
Flow control, 56, 57, 70
for loop, 70, 74
format(), 43
Function, 84, 86, 89, 92, 95, 96, 99
Functions, 56

Generative AI, 9
Google colaboratory, 8

Hierarchical function, 110

if, 57
if-elif-else, 62

if-else, 60
In-line comment, 10
Index, 37
input(), 16
int, 19
Interactive Python, 4
ipynb, 6

Jupyter Notebook, 2, 5–7
JupyterLab, 6

List, 119
List comprehension, 136
Logical operations, 26, 31
Loop, 70

Mapping, 170
Markdown, 7
Matplotlib, 5
Multiline comment, 13

Named tuple, 190, 191
namedtuple, 190, 191
Negative index, 38
Nested function, 107
NumPy, 5, 6

Operations, 26

Pandas, 5, 6
Parameter, 89
Plotly, 5
print(), 10
Python, 2, 3
Python 2, 3
Python 3, 3

Recursion, 112
Reference, 19
Relational operations, 26, 30
Repetition, 70

Return value, 99

Scikit-learn, 5, 6
Script Python, 4
Seaborn, 5
Set, 158
Space complexity, 187
Static typing, 21
str, 36

String, 2, 10, 11, 19, 36
String slicing, 40

Time complexity, 187
Truth table, 32
Tuple, 143

Variable, 19, 21

while loop, 70